WE THE PEOPLE

VS. U.S. CONGRESS UNFAIR LAWS

THE SPIRIT OF THE ANTI-CHRIST

DR. WILLIAM L. SHEALS

WE THE PEOPLE
Dr. William L. Sheals

All rights reserved
Copyright © 2024 by Dr. William L. Sheals

Published by Spines Publishing Platform
ISBN: 979-8-89569-370-4

WE THE PEOPLE

CONTENTS

WE THE PEOPLE

"We the People of the United States, in Order to form a more perfect Union, establish Justice, insure domestic

Tranquility, provide for the common defense, promote the general Welfare, and secure the Blessings of Liberty to ourselves and our Posterity, do ordain and establish this Constitution for the United States of America."

- - PREAMBLE OF THE
CONSTITUTION

[1]

WE THE PEOPLE VS. THE SUPREME COURT WORST RULINGS

INTRODUCTION

"The Honorable, the Chief Justice and the Associate Justices of the Supreme Court of the United States. Oyez! Oyez! Oyez! All persons having business before the Honorable, the Supreme Court of the United States, are admonished to draw near and give their attention, for the Court is now sitting. God save the United States and this Honorable Court."

This proclamation expects the court to

be noble, and vigilant, seeking divine protection and direction, while in return, the judiciary fails to exhibit respect for basic human rights, of the citizens it's meant to serve. Becoming a Supreme Court Justice isn't just some fancy title bestowed lightly but is a badge of honor earned through unwavering, principled behavior that **earns** the respect and confidence of the citizens it serves. However, it's confounding, that a career as prestigious as a Supreme Court Justice, has no prerequisite for any formal legal training to be appointed.

Additionally, there are no age or work requirements for this lifetime position. The bar is set too low for the height of this position. In fact, the sole guideline tied to the role is that the President will choose the nominee and the Senate will approve the nominee, allowing them to play by their own rules. How refreshing!

.   .   .

Surely, the Founding Fathers exhibited forethought by meticulously considering the future long-term implications of the United States framework and stability while penning the qualifications for a Supreme Court Justice. Without a doubt, they pondered the delightful dance of legal precedents and the whimsical twists of the law in the centuries to come.

Certainly, they were aware that these types of appointments would have a significant impact on the landscape of the Judiciary. It seems that the Founding Fathers would have more foresight, than not, to know handing over this decision to the President and Senate would likely open the floodgates to justice stacking.

The U.S. Supreme Court, often heralded for being the pinnacle of the judicial branch and for shaping the nation's legal framework, has issued several rulings that are widely considered to be the worst rulings in the Court's storied history. "The court of last resort," has become the court of no result, thanks to its flawed rulings and perceived partisanship. Partisanship shouldn't be the puppet master pulling the strings on Justices' decisions. Their decisions are to be guided by the good old Constitution. So, here we are, unveiling the real conundrum.

The Supreme Court, the nation's highest court, has an unwavering obligation to keep the scales of justice balanced by honoring legal precedent. Ensuring that everyone is subject to the law and that everyone is treated fairly! Its purpose isn't to champion liberal or conservative ideology but to protect the legal rights of individuals, maintain a system of checks and balances, and guarantee that justice wears the same uniform throughout the United States government.

In order to prevent political corruption and abuse at all tiers of government, from the federal and state levels, the Founding Fathers designated the Supreme Court to serve as a watchdog over the Constitution. The

Articles of Confederation laid the ground-work for a federal government, but its limitations prompted the framers to create the Constitution, which has weathered the storm as the republic's guiding document. There are now three powerhouse branches of government. The executive, legislative, and judicial branches, each with distinct powers and responsibilities, thanks to the new Constitution.

The judicial branch is responsible for interpreting laws, settling disputes, performing judicial reviews, monitoring legal procedures and justice, conducting constitutional review, and protecting citizens' rights. The Court consists of eight associate justices and one chief justice, all of whom have life-time appointments. They are nominated by the President and confirmed by the Senate. A justice's seat on the court can only be filled by retirement, resignation, death, removal, or impeachment. Their decisions impact the country and reflect how American culture is changing in terms of values and ideas.

Several landmark rulings have come to be regarded as the worst decisions ever made by the Supreme Court. These verdicts violate the values of justice, equality, and constitutional safeguards. The decisions made by the Supreme Court's nine justices have had and continue to have an influence on a wide range of problems, including social policy, constitutional interpretation, civil rights, and the rule of law. However, being a conservative or liberal justice has no place in the Supreme Court.

When the Supreme Court rules on policy rather than reading the law, it makes contentious rulings. From the late 1800s to the present, we will look at the worst Supreme Court decisions in history.

CASE 1: DRED SCOTT (1857)

The Dred Scott vs. Sanford case is the worst ruling in the history of the United States Supreme Court. In this case, the Court upheld racial inequality in the law, weakened the authority of the federal government, and contributed to the ongoing issue of slavery.

In an attempt to settle the issue once and for all, the Court's decisive 7-2 majority ruling, communicated that African Americans, regardless of whether they were enslaved or free, were not regarded as citizens of the United States. Therefore, they did not have the legal authority to file a lawsuit in federal court. This ruling came at a time of extreme national conflict over the issue of slavery. In the years leading up to the case, the country had become progressively divided over whether or not to expand slavery into the U.S.'s new territories. This racist sentiment conflicted with the dialed-down racist product of the 1820 Missouri Compromise law, written by Henry Clay of Kentucky, who served different times in both the House and the Senate.

Congress reached the Compromise agreement to maintain the balance and structure between free and slave states. The contentious ruling outlawed slavery in the Louisiana Territory north of the Missouri Compromise Line but allowed Missouri to become a slave state and enter the Union.

Dred Scott, his wife, Harriet Robinson, and two daughters, Eliza and Lizzie, were all enslaved by the same owner. The Scott family was initially owned by an Army surgeon named Dr. John Emerson. After Emerson's death, the Scotts' ownership was transferred to Emerson's widow, Eliza Emerson. Following her death, their ownership was transferred to John Sanford, the brother of Eliza Emerson.

Enslaved in Missouri, Dred Scott and his

family were taken to Illinois and the Wisconsin Territory while owned by Dr. John Emerson. Although Emerson took the Scotts to these free territories, it was common for slaveholders to travel with their enslaved people for labor rather than compassion. The Scott family lived in these free territories for several years with Dr. Emerson. Perhaps seeing what freedom looked like presented a deep nostalgia of expectation. However, stark reality proved otherwise.

After the death of Dr. John Emerson, the family was transported back to the slave state of Missouri, to serve now widow, Eliza Emerson. She passed away only three years after her husband. This led to the transfer of ownership to John Sanford, where the pursuit of Dred Scott's emancipation began. On behalf of himself and his family, Dred Scott filed a lawsuit to gain freedom on the grounds that his presence, over the years in free states and territories where slavery was illegal, should grant him his right to freedom.

In a 7-2 majority ruling, the Court, led by Chief Justice Roger B. Taney, vehemently denied Scott's claim, arguing that as an African American, whether enslaved or free, were inferior and were not citizens of the nation but property and did not have legal rights. He also added to the majority's position by affirming that Congress did not have the authority to ban slavery in federal territories. Taney concluded that the Missouri Compromise was unconstitutional, arguing that it violated the Fifth Amendment's protection of property rights by denying slaveholders the right to their **property** without providing them with due process of law.

Only a profoundly ingrained racist perspective regarding human beings could form out of the mouth of Chief Justice Taney's majority viewpoint. He was a protege of his predecessor, Chief John Marshall, whose wealthy family from Virginia, owned hundreds of enslaved African Americans.

Needless to say, the nation's very first chief justice was pro-slavery.

This type of racist rhetoric was a reflection of the prevalent beliefs of those who advocated for the institution, which opened the pathway for the expansion of slavery across all of the United States territories. But why wouldn't such honorable men be attentive to his needs and grant him freedom? Because enslaved people were the greatest source of wealth for white people and the greatest factor in the entire economic development of the United States of America in slave states. Enslaved African Americans had no freedom, worked for free, were forced into brutal labor conditions, were subjected to physical punishment, and sexual abuse, and were under the constant threat of violence to maintain their labor force. Therefore, by default, their forced, unpaid labor was the source of wealth for white slaveholders and their economic gain.

However, Justices John McLean and

Benjamin Curtis expressed dissension. The dissenting opinion of Justice Curtis was particularly noteworthy because he stated factually that free African Americans had been regarded as citizens in some states during the time that the Constitution was being written, and Dred Scott should have the legal right to file a lawsuit. Furthermore, he refuted Taney's assertion that Congress did not possess the jurisdiction to govern slavery in the territories. He countered by pointing out that Congress had, throughout the course of the nation's history, regulated slavery in a number of territories.

Following the ruling, the Republican Party emerged with the aim of curbing the spread of slavery. Abraham Lincoln was the first Republican president elected in 1860 to this newly formed party. He too voiced his disapproval of the decision. In the well-known "House Divided" address, Abraham Lincoln issued a warning that the nation could not tolerate "half slave and half free." Although he was initially focused on preserving the Union, his views evolved, leading to compassion that led to emancipation as a necessary step toward justice and unity. Regarded as having Christian values, perhaps he evolved from a cultural Christian to a Christian.

Although the ruling in the Dred Scott v. Sanford case strengthened the institution of slavery, it led to the Civil War. Subsequent to the Civil War, the Thirteenth, Fourteenth, and Fifteenth Amendments were ratified, extending citizenship and voting rights to all citizens of the United States, and ensuring that they would all be afforded equal protection under the law.

Slavery was a contentious issue in the United States and the ruling and overreach by the Supreme Court was the most reprehensible assault on the concepts of freedom and equality in the annals of American legal history.

CASE 2: PLESSY VS. FERGUSON (1896)

Another monumental Supreme Court decision was Plessy v. Ferguson, which upheld racial segregation on the grounds of "separate but equal." A man of mixed race named Homer Plessy deliberately provoked this case when he sat down in a "whites-only" train car in Louisiana to protest the state's segregation regulations. Plessy was found guilty of violating the segregation law when he refused to transfer to the other train car reserved for "colored" passengers. He took issue with the legislation and filed an appeal, claiming it ran afoul of the 14th Amendment's Equal Protection Clause. The Supreme Court's 7-1 ruling affirmed Plessy's conviction and established that "equal" segregation in state-run institutions was permissible. The ruling was 7-1, not 7-2 as Justice David J. Brewer was not present to participate due to a family bereavement at the time.

Considering the United States in the

years following Reconstruction will help provide light on the relevance of the Plessy v. Ferguson ruling. The Thirteenth, Fourteenth, and Fifteenth Amendments were ratified between 1865 and 1877, following the Civil War, with the objectives of outlawing slavery, guaranteeing equal legal protection, and granting voting rights to African American men.

The federal government attempted to help formerly enslaved African Americans become full members of American society during the Reconstruction era. But there was pushback to these initiatives, particularly the Ku Klux Klan and other white supremacist organizations in the South where state governments tried to reinstate white supremacy by passing "Jim Crow" laws that made segregation official.

There was a decline in federal support for African American civil rights in the nineteenth century, and some Southern states passed legislation to enforce segregation in public spaces, including schools, buses, and parks. Racial segregation was deemed permissible under these statutes on the grounds that providing equal access to facilities would not constitute an inherent form of discrimination.

For over fifty years following Plessy's decision, the legal basis for racial segregation was this concept, reflected in the doctrine of "separate but equal." A frontal challenge to the legal foundations of Jim Crow legislation was made in the Plessy case. The Supreme Court's decision to uphold Louisiana's segregation law effectively legitimized racial discrimination and further entrenched it as a fundamental aspect of American society, particularly in the South.

Justice Henry Billings Brown's majority ruling established the "separate but equal" theory, which would have a profound impact on American law and society for many years to come. The 14th Amendment, according to Brown, was meant to guarantee African

Americans legal and political equality, not social fairness. He insisted that segregation laws were based on the "established usages, customs, and traditions of the people" and did not suggest that African Americans were inherently inferior.

All people, regardless of race, are entitled to equal protection under the law, according to Justice John Marshall Harlan's argument that the Constitution is "color-blind." Justice Harlan accurately predicted that the Plessy judgment would have the same devastating impact as the Dred Scott decision; indeed, the decision laid the **legal** groundwork for decades of institutionalized racism. In hindsight, Justice Harlan's dissenting opinion was a prophetic attack on the erroneous logic of the Court. "Separate but equal" theory, he said, was a misrepresentation of the 14th Amendment and a horrible example that may lead to more discrimination in the name of equality in the law.

The ruling that upheld Jim Crow laws, which required segregation in practically all public activities, had a disastrous effect on African Americans, especially in the South. Black people were subjected to demeaning and inferior conditions as a result of segregation in many public spaces, including schools, public transit, bathrooms, restaurants, theaters, and even water fountains. The reality of tangibility was drastically different from the Court's conclusion that segregation did not inevitably mean inferiority. Overcrowding, poor maintenance, and lack of funding plagued most "colored" institutions. For instance, in the South, black schools were more likely to be located in run-down structures, have less funding, and employ fewer competent educators than their white counterparts.

Additionally, these inequalities were mirrored in the housing market and public transit, as African Americans were compelled to reside in substandard homes and segregated communities with inadequate amenities.

Not only did this ruling bring attention to economic inequality, but it also helped to establish the perception that African Americans were again regarded as second-class citizens and could be legitimately excluded from participating in American public life. Legalizing segregation institutionalized the view of Black people as inferior, which in turn legitimized racist attitudes and denied African Americans' equal opportunities. For a long time, it appeared that the civil rights struggle was a waste of time. Fighting segregation or exercising the 14th Amendment rights under a legal system that had affirmed it as constitutional was an uphill battle for African Americans. However, decisions such as Brown v. Board of Education (1954) began the Supreme Court's dismantling of the legal framework that Plessy had established in the mid-twentieth century.

Plessy v. Ferguson is among the worst

Supreme Court rulings. This case stands out for a number of reasons. To start, the decision firmly established racial segregation, which deprived African Americans of equal opportunities in areas like housing, education, and work. The institutionalization of racism and the systematic denial of advancements and opportunities for African Americans were both fostered by the law of segregation. Additionally, the argument by the Court in the case was severely incorrect. The concept that segregated facilities could ever be equal disregards the fact that racism is a serious problem in the United States.

Plessy's decision upheld a racial caste structure and white supremacy, both of which denied African Americans full citizenship rights. Thirdly, American society was severely and permanently impacted by the verdict. Jim Crow laws, which maintained the legal, social, and economic subjugation of African Americans for over 50 years, had Plessy as its legal basis. Restrictive housing covenants and job discrimination are two further examples of institutional racism that the decision upheld. Lastly, by arguing that segregation was constitutional, Plessy slowed down the movement for racial equality. Brown v. Board of Education, a seminal judgment that rejected the "separate but equal" doctrine in 1954, was the first step in the civil rights movement -an almost sixty-year effort to reverse Plessy's damage towards African Americans.

CASE 3: BUCK VS. BELL (1927)

In the annals of American legal history, Buck v. Bell is arguably one of the most dark and shameful rulings of the Supreme Court. Under the guise of pseudoscience, the most powerful court in the land, outwitted by the devil, sanctioned the violation of fundamental human rights, caused unimaginable pain to thousands of individuals, and perpetuated toxic ideas of ableism and racism. The decision's impact serves as a clear reminder of the perils of permitting prejudice over sound judicial judgments and the need to protect individual rights, specifically for the most vulnerable members of society.

In 1927, the Supreme Court ruling of Buck v. Bell affirmed the legality of Virginia's state law that permitted forced sterilization of those who were considered "unfit" to create offspring. Carrie Buck, a young woman placed in an institution, was ordered to undergo sterilization because she was considered "feebleminded" and because she came from a family with perceived mental disabilities.

In an astounding 8-1 decision, the Court, in an opinion issued by Justice Oliver Wendell Holmes, determined that the state's interest in avoiding the birth of "socially inadequate offspring" permitted sterilization. More heinously, the Court declared that "three generations of imbeciles were enough." Pierce Butler, the only dissenting justice in the case, opposed eugenics on moral and religious grounds.

A more comprehensive understanding of the eugenics movement, which was gaining prominence in the early 20th century, is required in order to comprehend the conclusion that was made in this particular case. Eugenics, a pseudoscience that was founded on the assumption that the human race might be improved by regulating reproduction, was generally supported by a large number of scientists, legislators, and social reformers throughout this time period. It was maintained by proponents of eugenics that society might be improved by preventing persons with what are considered to be inherited abnormalities, such as mental illness or intellectual disability, from having children.

During this period, many states approved laws authorizing the forced sterilization of those deemed "unfit" to reproduce. People with mental disorders, the impoverished, and members of racial minorities were frequently the targets of these laws. These laws were justified on the basis that they would improve public health and reduce the strain that would be placed on public welfare services. The sterilization statute of Virginia, which was passed in 1924, gave the state the authority to sterilize those who were confined to institutions due to mental illness or disability, which was upheld for decades.

One of the people who fell prey to the eugenics regulations that were in effect during that time period was Carrie Buck. Carrie was sent to the Virginia State Colony for Epileptics and Feebleminded after she was raped by her foster parent's nephew, J.T. Dobbs, and became pregnant at the age of 17. These events led to her placement in the institution and eventual sterilization.

Carrie Buck was from a family that was economically disadvantaged. In light of the fact that both her mother and her child were deemed to be "feebleminded" by the state, the decision was made to sterilize her. It was the belief of the state that sterilization was necessary in order to forestall the birth of "defective" offspring in succeeding generations. Carrie was unsuccessful in her attempt to appeal the sterilization order on the grounds that it violated her constitutional rights. In the end, she was unable to convince the court to reverse the order. Ultimately, the Supreme Court decided against her.

The dominant idea of eugenics at the time was reflected in the majority ruling, written by Justice Holmes. Through his argument, Holmes contended that the state had a valid interest in preventing individuals who were born with congenital disorders from passing on those characteristics to subsequent generations. He presented sterilization as a type of public health intervention, using parallels between it and mandatory vaccination to illustrate his point. In the same way that the government may mandate that individuals receive vaccinations in order to stop the spread of illness, it could likewise sterilize individuals in order to stop the spread of "genetic defects."

The opinion of Justice Holmes rejected the notion that the 14th Amendment's due process rights were violated by the practice of sterilization upon individuals. As a result of Carrie being afforded a hearing and the procedure had already been carried out in accordance with the rules of the state, Holmes contended that her rights had not been infringed.

In addition to this, he said that the freedom of individuals to exercise reproductive autonomy was subordinate to the interest of society in expanding the gene pool. "Three generations of imbeciles are enough," Justice Holmes said in his opinion. Referring to Carrie, her mother, and her daughter, all of whom were labeled by the state despite little evidence to support the claim. Before her untimely death, Vivian, Carrie's daughter, was a typical student in school and did not exhibit any evidence of an intellectual disability.

In the decades that followed the decision in Buck v. Bell, thousands of vulnerable people were subjected to forced sterilization. This ruling was disastrous for many individuals. A legal precedent for eugenics legislation across the United States was established as a result of this majority opinion, which effectively gave states the green light to continue sterilizing individuals who were judged "unfit" to reproduce. Over sixty thousand individuals were sterilized as a result of these regulations prior to the mid-20th century when the practice of forced sterilization became less popular.

As a result of the ruling, the perceptions of individuals with disabilities, the poor, and racial minorities in American society were altered in a more widespread manner. The Supreme Court endorsed the notion that certain individuals were innately inferior and should be kept from reproducing by considering forced sterilization to be an acceptable public health intervention. In addition to providing a justification for the infringement of individual rights, this way of thinking was also a contributing factor in the pervasive discrimination that was directed at individuals who were disabled, those who were poor, and those who were deemed "unfit" by the norms of society.

Not only did the ruling in Buck v. Bell have an impact within the United States, but it also had implications on a global scale. Nazi Germany used the verdict as justification for its own eugenics programs, which involved the coercive sterilization of hundreds of thousands of individuals that ultimately resulted in the Holocaust. The ruling was approved by Nazi Germany. The Buck v. Bell legacy is characterized by a number of gloomy characteristics, one of the most ominous being the relationship between American eugenics and Nazi philosophy.

Buck v. Bell has never been formally overturned by the Supreme Court, despite the fact that laws requiring forced sterilization were eventually abolished or abandoned in the majority of states. However, other decisions, such as Skinner v. Oklahoma (1942), which dealt with the sterilization of criminals, have put doubt on the ongoing validity of Buck as a precedent.

In addition, there is evidence that recent sterilization abuses have occurred in the United States, affecting persons who are jailed. The results of investigations have shown instances in which women, particularly those incarcerated, were sterilized without the appropriate level of informed consent. By way of illustration, in the year 2020, there were allegations that undocumented women were being sterilized against their will in ICE detention camps. In addition, an investigation of incidents that occurred in California jails found that more than 140 women were sterilized between the years 2006-2010 without the appropriate authority or consent. These events bring to light the continuous problems that individuals who are jailed face with in relation to their reproductive rights.

Many states issued public apologies for their sterilization programs in the decades that followed the ruling, and some states instituted compensation programs for those who survived the practice of forced sterilization. The state of Virginia, which is at the core of the Buck case, issued a public apology in 2002 for its involvement in the eugenics movement. In 2015, the state established a compensation fund for the survivors who were still alive at the time.

A number of factors contribute to the widespread consensus that Buck v. Bell is among the worst decisions ever handed down by the Supreme Court. A violation of the basic rights of individuals to make decisions about their own bodies and reproductive rights was the first consequence of the finding. Thousands of people were denied their autonomy and exposed to severe abuse of power as a result of the Supreme Court's decision to preserve the states' ability to sterilize people illegally and without their permission.

The decision was formed on the basis of eugenicist philosophy and research that were severely faulty. The eugenics movement, which aimed to improve society by limiting reproduction, has been largely rejected as a pseudoscience that has its roots in racism, ableism, and classism. Buck v. Bell is now considered as an example of how prejudice and pseudoscience may corrupt legal thinking. The premise that certain individuals were genetically "inferior" and therefore be prohibited from reproducing has been rejected by current science, and the judgment in Buck v. Bell today is seen as an example of how this can happen.

The decision was a factor in the long-standing pattern of discrimination and abuse of individuals with disabilities, the vulnerable, and populations that are marginalized. People with intellectual and physical impairments were portrayed as a burden on society and denied fundamental human rights as a result of the ruling, which perpetuated damaging stereotypes about these individuals. It also created the framework for future abuses, such as the forced sterilization of minority groups, notably women of color, in the United States long into the 20th century. ADD MORE. The opportunity to have children and to live their lives according to their own terms was denied to these women, and the emotional and psychological toll of forced sterilization continues to afflict survivors and their descendants to this day.

CASE 4: KOREMATSU VS. THE UNITED STATES (1944)

Set within the backdrop of WWII and the pervasive anti-Japanese sentiment that followed the bombing of Pearl Harbor, the Korematsu case became clear of the long-standing racial prejudice and blatant racism against Asian immigrants and the judiciary failure to protect their constitutional rights even in the time of war.

This case is at the center of the legal question, of whether or not Executive Order 9066, which authorized the incarceration of primarily Japanese Americans during World War II, with the absence of proof of guilt was within the bounds of the law. In a 6-3 majority ruling, the Supreme Court rationalized yet another contentious judgment by ruling against Fred Korematsu, upholding the government's actions as constitutional. The majority ruling, written by Justice Hugo Black, established that the need to protect against espionage exceeded Korematsu's individual freedoms. The Court ruled that the exclusion and internment orders were a military necessity during wartime and were not based on racial prejudice.

Following the attack that Japan launched on Pearl Harbor, the U.S. government became increasingly concerned about national security on the West Coast. Fear and paranoia over potential espionage or sabotage by people of Japanese descent, whether citizens or non-citizens, led to President Franklin D. Roosevelt issuing Executive Order 9066. This order gave the military the power to exclude people from certain areas of the country and declare them military zones, effectively sanctioning the forced relocation and internment of "any or all persons," but primarily 120,000 Japanese Americans, the majority of whom were U.S. citizens, to internment camps.

U.S. citizen Fred Korematsu, of Japanese descent, was arrested and convicted for refusing to leave his San Leandro, California home. He asserted his rights under the Fifth Amendment to contest the internment regime. Claiming Japanese American incarceration violated their constitutional rights. The Supreme Court rejected Korematsu's claims, ruling that the internment was lawful due to "emergency and peril."

Although there were no measures used against Italian or German Americans during this war, the internment of Japanese Americans illustrates that of racial prejudice, a common theme in American history. The internment policy had widespread support and was rationalized as necessary for national security, even though there was no proof of Japanese American espionage or sabotage. Since the case failed to challenge the government's presumptions on the allegiance of Japanese Americans, the 6-3 majority opinion was severely defective in its acceptance of the internment's rationale.

The ruling established a worrying precedent for the suspension of civil freedoms during times of crisis, thereby giving the government considerable flexibility to violate individual rights during warfare.

Justice Frank Murphy disagreed, describing the ruling as an egregious breach of the Constitution. He said that "racial antagonism" rather than a genuine military need underpinned the internment strategy. According to Murphy, the internment of Japanese Americans was motivated more by racism than by legitimate security concerns, and there was zero proof of betrayal on the part of Japanese Americans.

Justice Robert Jackson joined the other justices in dissenting, expressing concern that the ruling would set a harmful precedent that could enable future racial or ethnic profiling by the government in the name of national security. During times of war, Jackson contended, the courts should not submit so fully to the government, particularly when basic constitutional rights were at risk.

This ruling dismantled the constitutional safeguards that all people were promised and gave the government permission to discriminate against certain races. The Supreme Court once again endorsed one of the most heinous abuses of civil rights in American history. The ruling was a cautionary tale about the perils of unbridled government authority in times of crises and the precarious position minority groups find themselves in when the state acts out of bigotry and fear.

However, a lower federal court overturned Korematsu's conviction in 1983 following the disclosure that the government had suppressed crucial evidence throughout the Supreme Court case. The government's records revealed that the military had inflated the threat of Japanese Americans in order to rationalize the internment and that no solid proof of espionage or sabotage existed among Japanese Americans.

A public apology and financial compensation were granted to the surviving Japanese Americans who had been incarcerated under the Civil Liberties Act of 1988, which Congress had enacted in the previous year, recognizing that "racial prejudice, wartime hysteria, and a failure of political leadership" had driven the internment. Chief Justice John Roberts stated that the Korematsu judgment was "gravely wrong the day it was decided," and had "no place in law under the Constitution."

Because it once again justified a program of mass detention and racial discrimination based on irrational concerns and prejudice, Korematsu v. United States is among the worst Supreme Court judgments ever. The Court's failure to investigate the government's assertions of "military necessity" and its over-reliance on the executive branch during a crisis contributed to the erroneous thinking that underpinned this ruling.

By implying that all persons of Japanese ancestry, regardless of their citizenship or allegiance to the United States, were intrinsically suspicious, the Korematsu decision legitimized racial discrimination and furthered racial stereotypes. Japanese Americans suffered terrible repercussions as a result of this, including the loss of their houses, companies, and personal liberties as a result of incarceration and the continuation of prejudice even after the war ended. Even in times of national catastrophe, it is crucial to protect civil rights, especially in the face of unbridled government authority. Prejudice and fear should never be allowed to supersede constitutional safeguards.

CASE 5: AFFIRMATIVE ACTION CASES (1978-2023)

"Affirmative Action" refers to policies and practices that are intended to increase opportunities for groups who have been historically excluded, notably in sectors such as education and employment. The purpose of these policies is to rectify prejudice that has occurred in the past and to guarantee that minorities, women, and other underrepresented groups are represented fairly.

In 1965, President Lyndon B. Johnson signed Executive Order 11246 which laid the groundwork for the implementation of affirmative action. He was a Texan who had grown up in poverty and went on to become a seasoned leader in Congress. In addition, prior to his administration tenure, he was elected to the House of Representatives and became the majority leader of the Senate. According to his executive order, government contractors were obligated to implement "affirmative action" in order to guarantee that employees are treated without regard to factors such as race, color, religion, sex, or national origin. The directive was essential in laying the groundwork for affirmative action in employment and, later, in education.

There have been several rulings that have set back the efforts to promote diversity and address historical systemic racism in education. Ninety-nine percent of these cases have been White students against affirmative action but a more recent case has included White and Asian students against affirmative action. Considering history, it is reprehensible that Congress, over time, left a system that could be challenged and questioned under any claim. This hodgepodge of scrutinizing perspectives has made affirmative action the scapegoat for students who did not get accepted into their college of choice. The idea that race-conscious admissions processes benefit underrepresented minority students at the expense of other students is the source of this notion. This perception frequently results in allegations of "reverse discrimination" being made by candidates who are white or Asian American. Nevertheless, the truth is more complicated than the assumption.

There is no denying the fact that college admissions are extremely difficult, particularly at prestigious educational institutions. Tens of thousands of applications are submitted to Ivy League schools, while only a few thousand slots are available for admission. A significant number of students who possess exceptional qualifications, irrespective of their racial or ethnic background, are not granted admission due to the sheer number of applications received and the restricted number of available spots. It is a common misunderstanding that affirmative action policies involve racial quotas or admit students solely based on their ethnicity regardless of their qualifications, who are not qualified only on the basis of their race.

The Supreme Court ruled against quotas in favor of Bakke in the case of Regents of the University of California v. Bakke (1978). Subsequent decisions like Grutter v. Bollinger (2003) and Fisher v. University of Texas (2016) reinforced the idea and highlighted that race-conscious admissions must be tightly restricted and utilized as part of a holistic examination. This indicates that the use of affirmative action was never the only factor considered when deciding whether or not to admit a student. Furthermore, research has shown that the majority of students who were refused would not have been accepted even if there had been no affirmative action in place. Students and their parents are likely to seek answers for the rejection of an application from a psychological standpoint. This is especially true in situations when the student has solid academic credentials. Because affirmative action is a policy that is out in the open and contentious, students may assume that it has a direct impact on their prospects of being accepted into college. This can make it an easy target for discontent.

It is unfortunate that every time African Americans have made progress in this world, there is a setback from people who feel superior, the courts and legislature, who not only uphold this absurdity but who turn back the hand of time.

While they share a common theme of narrowing the permissible scope of affirmative action, often under the guise of "equal protection" or preventing "reverse discrimination," the implications of these rulings are far-reaching.

However, there is a more recent case, The Students for Fair Admissions vs. Harvard and University of North Carolina (2023), that deserves more focus because it is the ruling that has marked the end of progress made since the Civil Rights Movement, which addressed racial inequalities in education.

In the years leading up to the Supreme Court's ruling challenging the validity of race-conscious admissions methods, the debate over affirmative action heated up.

Finally, the ruling came after years of legal challenges claiming that affirmative action adversely impacts white or Asian American applicants.

The landmark ruling in Students for Fair Admissions v. Harvard and University of North Carolina (UNC) in June 2023 by the Supreme Court significantly changed affirmative action policies in US higher education. This ruling broke a decades-long precedent by prohibiting racial factors in college admissions. Students for Fair Admissions (SFFA), an advocacy organization founded by conservative legal strategist Edward Blum, filed two cases that influenced the conclusion taken in response to both complaints. By discriminating against Asian

American and White candidates, the Student Federalist Association (SFFA) claimed that Harvard and UNC's affirmative action policies violated Title VI of the Civil Rights Act of 1964 (which applies to private institutions like Harvard) and the Equal Protection Clause of the Fourteenth Amendment.

A conservative majority of the Supreme Court ruled in favor of the Student Financial Aid Act (SFFA), thereby putting an end to the use of affirmative action in college admissions. The judgment was evenly divided along ideological lines. The decision was handed down, with a vote of 6-3 in the case involving the University of North Carolina and a vote of 6-2 in the case involving Harvard (Justice Ketanji Brown Jackson recused herself from the Harvard case owing to her previous participation on the board of representatives of the university).

In the majority decision, Chief Justice John Roberts noted that the admissions systems at Harvard and UNC violated the

Equal Protection Clause because they lacked "sufficiently focused and measurable objectives." This was the main argument that was made in the ruling. The Court came to the conclusion that the use of race in these programs was not narrowly tailored, which means that it did not meet the rigorous scrutiny standard that is necessary for policies that use racial classifications when they are implemented.

Beginning with Bakke, the ruling overturned a legal precedent that had been in place for forty-five years.

The opinion of the majority was supported by a number of other justices, including Clarence Thomas, Samuel Alito, Neil Gorsuch, Brett Kavanaugh, and Amy Coney Barrett. A concurring opinion was made by Clarence Thomas, who had benefitted from affirmative action fifty-four years prior. In this opinion, he opposed affirmative action, stating that it is fundamentally discriminatory and ineffectual. His concurring opinion disregards the historical institutional racism that has existed throughout history and does not take into account the larger experiences of other oppressed minorities who have benefited from race-sensitive measures without experiencing the same sense of stigmatization.

Sonia Sotomayor, Elena Kagan, and Ketanji Brown Jackson, the three liberal justices of the Supreme Court, each submitted their dissenting opinion. The ruling, according to Justice Sotomayor, "rolls back decades of progress" and contradicts the nation's commitment to equality, as she stated in a vehement dissent to the decision. It was her contention that regulations regarding admissions that take into account racial factors are essential in order to combat the ongoing inequality that exists in American society and to encourage diversity in the educational system.

As part of her dissenting opinion in the case involving the University of North Carolina, Justice Jackson noted that the conclusion made by the majority was "ahistorical" and overlooked the fact that racism is a pervasive problem in the United States. Affirmative action programs are essential to addressing long-standing inequalities, she claimed, and it is impossible to separate the concept of race from the reality of the person.

Therefore, colleges are prohibited from using race as a criterion for admission, which will lead to a decrease in the number of underrepresented minority students enrolling in prestigious universities. This was seen in areas like Michigan and California, where affirmative action was formerly outlawed at the state level, resulting in a sharp decline in the number of African American and Latino students enrolling in public colleges. In order to preserve diversity, universities are now required to investigate racial-neutral alternatives, such as emphasizing socioeconomic aspects, increasing outreach to mar-

ginalized   populations,   or   providing
scholarships to deserving students.

Although affirmative action was established to promote diversity, rather than place
one group at a disadvantage over the others,
it is frequently blamed for students being
denied admission to their preferred institutions, it is generally just one of numerous
elements in a multifaceted admissions
framework. The role it plays in admissions is
to foster a diverse educational environment;
however, attributing individual rejections to
this aspect simplifies the complex and com-
petitive landscape of college admissions. Ad-
ditional factors, including institutional
priorities, legacy preferences, and geograph-
ical diversity, frequently exert a more significant influence on the admissions process.
While affirmative action may serve as a con-
venient rationale for feelings of disappoint-
ment, it is improbable that it constitutes the
exclusive factor influencing an individual
student's denial of admission. Nonetheless,

the legislation and executive directives that originally endorsed affirmative action, including Executive Order 11246 and Title VII of the Civil Rights Act of 1964, continue to hold considerable importance in the realms of employment and contracting, as the ruling by Students for Fair Admissions is focused specifically on college admissions. Title VI persists in prohibiting explicit racial discrimination.

CASE 6: BRNOVICH VS. DEMOCRATIC NATIONAL COMMITTEE (2021)

African American men earned the right to vote following the ratification of the 15th Amendment to the U.S. Constitution in 1870. This amendment prohibited the unlawful denial of voting rights on the basis of race, color, or prior state of slavery. African American women attained full voting rights in 1920; yet, they encountered the same barriers as African American males, as states instituted barriers such as literacy tests, poll fees, and intimidation to discourage African Americans from voting. The discriminatory practices were officially prohibited after the March in Selma, Alabama, and the enactment of the Voting Rights Act in 1965, which provided greater protection for African American voting rights.

The persistent issue of voting rights has emerged prominently due to a voter registration push initiated by civil rights activists in Selma, Alabama. Of Selma's "15,000" black citizens eligible to vote, just "335" were registered. On March 7, 1965, "600" civil rights activists set out to march from Selma to the state capital of Montgomery. On the event referred to as "Bloody Sunday," they were confronted by law enforcement utilizing tear gas, batons, and whips. Media coverage of the tragic events horrified and motivated Americans across the nation to travel to Alabama in solidarity, climaxing in a march to Montgomery on March 25, 1965, attended by approximately 25,000 individuals, under the leadership of Dr. Martin Luther King, Jr., and shielded by U.S. troops, the National Guard, and the FBI. Currently, that path is recognized as the U.S. National Historic Trail.

On August 4, 1965, the United States Senate passed the Voting Rights Act. However, it was not until August 6, 1965, following extensive deliberations between the House and Senate on the bill, that President Johnson signed the Voting Rights Act into law. Johnson said that the legislation sprang from a "clear and simple injustice," and its purpose was "to correct that injustice." The "outrage of Selma" prompted a response from the federal government, and the efforts of the bipartisan Senate Judiciary Committee supported the victory of political equality for the previously disenfranchised through the ballot.

The Voting Rights Act (VRA), passed on August 6, 1965, has undergone five amendments from 1970 to 2006. These amendments collectively demonstrate Congress's continuous attempts to modify the Voting Rights Act in response to the evolving dynamics of voting discrimination in the U.S., enhancing protections for minority and linguistic groups (citizens with low English proficiency) and addressing judicial challenges. Subsequent to the Shelby County decision in 2013 and the two-term election of President Barack Obama, the effectiveness of the Voting Rights Act has been significantly weakened, especially concerning the preclearance provisions.

Section 5 of the Voting Rights Act established a preclearance requirement, requiring that specific states and local jurisdictions with a history of racial discrimination in voting obtain federal approval, or "preclearance," prior to enacting any modifications to their voting laws or procedures. The approval may be granted by either the U.S. Department of Justice or the U.S. District Court for the District of Columbia.

Preclearance was implemented in jurisdictions, primarily in the South, namely, Alabama, Georgia, Louisiana, Mississippi, South Carolina, Virginia, and more recently Arizona, Texas, Florida, North Carolina, Wisconsin, Pennsylvania, Ohio, and Iowa—that exhibited a documented history of voting discrimination in regions with historically low voter turnout or registration among minorities, where discriminatory measures, such as literacy exams, served as obstacles to voting. Prior to implementing modifications to voting practices, including redistricting, altering polling locations, adjusting voter ID requirements, or revising registration procedures, covered jurisdictions were required to demonstrate that such changes would not discriminate against minority voters or exacerbate their circumstances.

Preclearance was intended to prevent states and municipalities with a history of prejudice from passing legislation that would disenfranchise black voters. It successfully served as a preventative measure, preventing discriminatory legislation from taking effect rather than needing minority organizations to contest such laws after they were passed. Preclearance was originally intended to last five years when the VRA was approved in 1965, but it has been renewed and extended multiple times through modifications, with the most recent extension in 2006 for another 25 years.

However, in Shelby County v. Holder (2013), the Supreme Court invalidated Section 4(b), the mechanism for determining which areas were subject to preclearance, essentially rendering Section 5 unenforceable. The Court argued that the coverage technique was out of date since it was based on the 1960s and 1970s statistics and Congress had not revised it to reflect modern conditions. As a result, unless Congress changes the formula, no jurisdictions are required to get preclearance.

This takes us to the Brnovich v. Democratic National Committee lawsuit in 2021. This is a key Supreme Court case that addresses the applicability of Section 2 of the Voting Rights Act of 1965 (VRA) and how it relates to state voting restrictions. The case centered on two Arizona voting practices that were challenged by the Democratic National Committee (DNC), which contended that the restrictions unfairly burdened minority voters and so violated the VRA.

The two main concerns challenged were Arizona's out-of-precinct policy, which states that ballots cast in the incorrect precinct would be destroyed regardless of the voter's ability to vote in other contests on the ballot.

Second, the ballot collection prevents third-party individuals (other than family members, caretakers, or election officials) from gathering and delivering another person's completed ballot.

Section 2 of the Voting Rights Act of 1965 (VRA) is one of the most essential components of the law since it prohibits discriminatory voting methods or processes based on race, color, or membership in a minority language group.

Unlike Section 5 of the VRA, which required certain jurisdictions with a history of discrimination to seek federal approval before modifying their voting rules, Section 2 applies worldwide and offers a legal means for challenging discriminatory voting practices in court.

The DNC maintained that these restrictions disproportionately impacted minority votes, particularly Native American, Hispanic, and African American groups. They argued that minority voters in Arizona were more likely to vote outside of their precincts because of factors such as greater rates of housing instability or limited transportation availability. They further claimed that minority voters were more inclined to use third-party ballot collecting owing to obstacles such as rural distances or a lack of access to postal services. The Supreme Court ruled in favor of Mark Brnovich, then-Arizona Attorney General, preserving the state's voting restrictions. The court determined that neither of the challenged voting rules violated Section 2 of the VRA.

The majority ruling, written by Justice Samuel Alito, provided new principles for how courts should evaluate challenges to voting regulations under Section 2. Alito noted that Section 2 of the VRA is intended to ban racial discrimination in voting practices or legislation, but he limited the scope of how courts could interpret Section 2 to voting limitations.

He claimed that Section 2 should not be viewed too liberally and that simple statistical variations in how legislation affects different ethnic groups do not always imply a breach of Section 2. Instead, the question should be whether the laws make it "equally open" for voters of all races to vote in elections. The majority judgment established a set of guidelines for analyzing whether a voting law imposes an unreasonable hardship or a "substantial obstacle" on minority voters under Section 2 of the VRA. Alito contended that a law only violates the VRA if it imposes a significant impediment on a voter's capacity to participate in elections.

Alito outlined factors that courts should consider when determining whether a voting legislation violates the VRA. The hardship imposed by the rule. The extent to which the regulation deviates from typical voting patterns. Whether voting restrictions disproportionately affect racial and ethnic minorities. Whether the state has other voting options. The robustness of the state's reason for the legislation, such as the necessity to prevent fraud or ensuring that elections go smoothly. He pointed out that states are not bound to enhance voting convenience, and small obstacles do not constitute an unreasonable hardship under Section 2.

The Court's decision ignores the fact that voter suppression usually takes place through subtle strategies rather than overt discrimination. The DNC demonstrated that Arizona's Out-of-Precinct Voting Policy and Ballot Collection Ban disproportionately impacted Native American, Hispanic, and Black voters, who were more likely to cast ballots in the wrong precinct or rely on third-party ballot collection due to social and economic challenges. These behaviors may not appear discriminatory on the surface, but their varying impact on minority groups is obvious. By rejecting the idea that statistical evidence of varying impact might show a violation of Section 2, the Court essentially allowed rules that look neutral but consistently condemn voters of color.

Despite the absence of substantial evidence that voter fraud was a significant issue in Arizona, the Court granted unwarranted importance to Arizona's argument that these restrictions were essential to prevent voter fraud. The Ballot Collection Ban, in particular, had a disproportionate impact on rural Native American electors who are geographically isolated and have limited access to postal services, necessitating third-party assistance. However, the Court maintained the prohibition due to its conjecture apprehensions regarding fraud. This decision establishes a perilous precedent by permitting states to implement restrictive legislation under the pretense of preventing fraud, without necessitating that they provide concrete evidence that such legislation is necessary.

The Brnovich ruling will exacerbate the difficulty minority voters face in participating in elections, particularly as states implement more stringent voting laws. The Court has effectively undermined the Voting Rights Act, a law that has long been a critical safeguard against discriminatory voting practices, by upholding Arizona's laws. This decision implies that minor obstacles to voting are permissible, even when they disproportionately affect racial and ethnic minority communities. Consequently, states are now more empowered to implement voting restrictions that may further marginalize already vulnerable communities and reduce minority voter turnout.

CASE 7: DOBBS VS JACKSON WOMEN'S HEALTH ORGANIZATION (2022) IN THE OVERTURNING OF ROE VS WADE (1973)

A woman's constitutional right to an abortion was overturned by the Supreme Court of the United States. The Court's decision has once again challenged the Constitution's guarantee of women's liberty and equality. Prior to the adoption of this legal precedent in 2022, the majority of abortion cases were thrown out due to Roe v. Wade.

Nevertheless, an increasing number of

US states are enacting severe limitations on abortion, such as the heartbeat ban, which prohibits the operation after six weeks. Given that some women might not be aware that they are pregnant at the time, they can be stripped of their freedom of choice. As for the US Supreme Court, honestly, what can we truly expect from Congress at this point?

First, let us revisit the 1973 case of Roe v. Wade. Jane Roe(Norma McCorvey), was pregnant and wanted an abortion.

However, she lived in Texas, where abortions were prohibited. Henry Wade, the district attorney of Dallas County, Texas, implemented the Texas statute that restricted abortion to cases when a woman's life was at risk. Sarah Weddington and Linda Coffee submitted this case to the Court on behalf of Jane Roe, who was expecting her third child. Roe considered an abortion in Texas, where it was illegal unless necessary to save the mother's life. Sarah Weddington and Linda Coffee, her lawyers, sued Henry Wade, the local district attorney, in U.S. federal court. Citing that Texas's abortion laws violated constitutional principles. In 1969, The U.S. Federal Court in Northern Texas assessed the case, ruling in Jane Roe's favor. The ruling was appealed to the Supreme Court.

In January 1973, the Supreme Court issued a 7–2 majority ruling also in favor of Roe, concluding that excessively restrictive state regulation of abortion is unconstitutional. Through the Due Process Clause of the 14th Amendment's right to privacy, the Court upheld a woman's right to an abortion.

This Amendment guarantees a fundamental "right to privacy," protecting a pregnant woman's ability to terminate her pregnancy. The court concluded that abortion rights must be balanced with the government's interests in women's health and prenatal life. A trimester framework was established to reconcile conflicting goals in US abortion rules. The Court established the right to an abortion as "fundamental," necessitating that courts evaluate disputed abortion laws under the "strict scrutiny" standard, the most rigorous form of judicial review in the United States.

The United States Constitution's First Amendment establishes the separation of church and state. The Establishment Clause of the First Amendment prohibits the government from creating a religion or preferentially endorsing one religion over another. This safeguards the freedom to practice or abstain from religion according to individual preference. The expression "separation of church and state" serves as a metaphor for the Establishment Clause. The concept started with Roger Williams, the founder of Rhode Island, who believed that governmental interference in the church would lead to its corruption. Thomas Jefferson is famous for employing the idea of a "wall of separation" between religion and state in a letter concerning the First Amendment.

The founders of the United States maintained that the separation of religion and state was the most effective means to safeguard the rights of all individuals. The outcome is a significant level of religious freedom and interfaith cohesion in the United States. To align humanity's moral compass with a nation's political compass, we must first collectively choose to adhere to one deity. The Bible states in Exodus 20:3 (KJV), "Thou shalt have no other gods before me." Implying that no other deity, whether real or fictitious, should compete with the singular true God, who is the sole entity of significance.

Therefore, as a nation, we must comply with the doctrines of Jesus. Luke 9:23 (KJV) states, "And he said to them all, if any man desires to follow me, let him deny himself, take up his cross daily, and follow me." Had we been a Christian nation, the Supreme Court's rejection of Roe v. Wade in 1973 may have been considered a just ruling. If

God had meant for man to dominate women instead of her husband ruling over her (Genesis 3:16), the rejection of Roe v. Wade in 1973 may have been considered a legitimate Supreme Court ruling.

Besides, not every woman on earth has a husband, and since Roe lacks a husband, this does not imply that she is represented by nine justices defaulting as her spouse. The husband's authority in marriage is unique, and knowing the obligations of leadership, responsibility, and accountability as ordained by God requires knowledge of Him and an understanding of His word. The role of a spouse in a marriage is not one of superiority. Therefore, a man's judgments about a woman's personal freedom are irrelevant.

Our self-identification should reflect Christ rather than mimic Satan and his hypocrisy. Historically, the worldwide consensus has defined women's duties as confined to domestic domains, primarily as wives, while public life was exclusively designated for men. In medieval Europe, women were prohibited from owning property, pursuing education, and engaging in public life. By the end of the 19th century in France, women were still required to cover their heads in public, yet in certain regions of Germany, a husband had the legal right to sell his wife. Until the early 20th century, women were prohibited from voting or holding political office in Europe and the vast majority of the United States, although several territories and states had previously granted women's suffrage prior to the enactment of federal legislation. Women were prohibited from engaging in business activities without the presence of a male representative, such as a father, brother, spouse, legal agent, or son.

Married women were unable to exert authority over their own children without their husbands' consent. Furthermore, women had restricted or no access to school and were predominantly excluded from several careers. In certain regions of the world, such limitations on women persist to this day.

This brings us back to Roe v. Wade. Regardless of whether the court's decision supported Roe on the grounds of civil rights or human rights, both are her exclusive entitlements and no male possesses the authority to deprive a woman of her rights because of perceived intellectual superiority. The Supreme Court's ruling in Roe v. Wade (1973) was a landmark judgment that legalized abortion in the United States. The Court concluded that a woman's right to choose an abortion is protected by the Constitution, specifically through the right to privacy established in the Due Process Clause of the 14th Amendment. The Court determined that the Constitution's implicit privacy provisions are broad enough to encompass a woman's decision about the termination of her pregnancy.

The right to privacy evolved from earlier

rulings that recognized confidentiality in family, marriage, and reproductive affairs, as demonstrated by Griswold v. Connecticut (1965), which upheld privacy in marriage decisions. The Court acknowledged that governmental entities possess a legitimate interest in protecting the health of the mother and the possible life of the fetus. The Court aimed at reconciling the rights of pregnant women with the interests of the state. The court established that a woman's right to choose an abortion is essential in the early stages of pregnancy; nevertheless, as the pregnancy progresses and fetal viability is attained, the state's interest in protecting potential life becomes more contentious. Nonetheless, it weighed these interests against a woman's liberty to make decisions regarding her own body.

During the first trimester of pregnancy, the choice to terminate should be left to the woman and her doctor, with little governmental intervention. During the second trimester, the state may control abortion operations purely for the mother's health. In the third trimester, after the fetus achieves "viability" (the point at which it may survive independently outside the womb, usually between 24 and 28 weeks), the state may impose abortion limits or prohibitions in order to safeguard the mother's life or health.

The case established that states may impose restrictions on abortion post-viability, the period at which the fetus might potentially live outside the womb, marking a significant milestone in abortion law. The Court ruled in favor of Roe, with a 7-2 decision, invalidating Texas laws that restricted abortion to instances when the mother's life was at risk. This verdict significantly impacted several state and federal abortion restrictions across the country.

In June 2022, the Supreme Court reversed two landmark decisions, Roe v. Wade (1973) and Planned Parenthood of Southeastern Pennsylvania v. Casey (1992), which both established and defended women's constitutional right to abortion services. The majority in Dobbs argued that Roe and Casey were wrongly determined, claiming that the Constitution has no mention of abortion and that the right to an abortion is not "deeply rooted" in the nation's historical and customary framework.

The landmark case Roe vs. Wade established the legality of an abortion in the United States by ruling that a woman's right to choose an abortion is constitutionally protected by the right to privacy guaranteed by the 14th Amendment's Due Process Clause. The decision in Roe vs. Wade established a constitutional right to an abortion before the end of the second trimester of pregnancy, which the Court regarded as the most common point of fetal viability. The Supreme Court's ruling in Planned Parenthood v. Casey upheld the fundamental principles of Roe v. Wade while significantly altering the legal framework around abortion rights.

The Court affirmed the constitutional right to abortion before fetal viability and introduced a new legal criterion for evaluating abortion restrictions, termed the undue hardship test. This judgment allowed states to implement further limitations on abortion while preserving a woman's right to choose, although in a more limited capacity than originally established by Roe. Casey argued that a state may impose limits on abortion, provided that such laws do not create substantial obstacles to a woman's right to choose an abortion prior to fetal viability. If state law establishes such obstacles, it conflicts with the Constitution by improperly restricting a woman's freedom of choice over her own body.

The case of Dobbs v. Jackson Women's Health Organization featured Mississippi law known as the Gestational Age Act, which prevented most abortions after 15 weeks of gestation, significantly before the fetal viability threshold set by Roe and Casey. The Court upheld the statute, rejecting the viability standard established by Roe. The court stated that laws banning pre-viability abortion are not intrinsically unlawful. The state argued that it may "prohibit elective abortions before viability," claiming that no element of constitutional text, structure, history, or tradition supports a right to abortion.

By erasing Roe and Casey, the Court transferred the authority to govern abortion to individual states. This allows states to develop their own abortion legislation, with some states opting to ban or severely restrict abortion, while others maintain or expand access to abortion services. The Supreme Court's ruling in Dobbs v. Jackson Women's Health Organization represents a significant regression in women's rights and a dismantling of established constitutional protections. Reversing Roe v. Wade and

Planned Parenthood v. Casey undermines the basic principles of liberty, privacy, and personal freedom that have been integral to the American legal system for decades. This ruling dismisses the precedent established over 50 years of adopted legislation, social dependence on reproductive rights, and its enormous impact on women's health, equality, and personal freedom.

The Dobbs ruling weakens the principle of stare decisis, which fosters legal stability via fidelity to precedent. Roe and Casey established a definitive constitutional framework that reconciles a woman's right to choose with the state's interest in potential life. These cases have shaped American society for over fifty years, enabling generations of women to make critical decisions regarding their lives, health, and futures with the assurance that their reproductive rights were safeguarded. Reversing such a ruling not only contradicts legal continuity but also compromises other privacy-related rights, such as access to contraception and marital equality, which are also subject to judicial reinterpretation.

The majority ruling in Dobbs relies on a narrow interpretation of the Constitution, concluding that abortion is not a protected right due to its absence of explicit language. This by far reflects poor justice. However, this viewpoint ignores the more fundamental right to privacy guaranteed by the 14th Amendment's Due Process Clause, which protects personal decisions about family, marriage, and procreation.

In Griswold v. Connecticut (1965), the Court determined that the right to contraception is encompassed within the right to privacy, and Roe appropriately identified a woman's choice to terminate a pregnancy as an essential aspect of this liberty. The Dobbs ruling subordinated women's rights to the caprices of state lawmakers, disregarding the principle that human liberty, encompassing physical autonomy, is not to be determined by majority opinion.

Additionally, by transferring abortion legislation to the states, the Court reinforces inequality. The capacity of women to have an abortion is increasingly determined by geographic location and financial means, disproportionately impacting low-income women, women of color, and residents of states with restrictive abortion laws. A wide range of women will be required to travel lengthy distances, endure financial difficulties, or resort to dangerous abortion procedures. The Court's ruling ignores the tangible consequences for women unable to successfully overcome these barriers, thereby trampling on their fundamental rights once more due to their socioeconomic status.

The Dobbs verdict ultimately threatens women's health and welfare. Medical professionals have long warned that restrictive abortion rules elevate maternal mortality rates and endanger the lives of women with complicated pregnancies. The ruling permits states to ban abortion, therefore endangering access to safe and legal medical procedures and compelling women to resort to risky alternatives. This not only jeopardizes women's physical health but also hinders them from making crucial decisions regarding their families, careers, and personal lives. This decision constitutes a substantial misjudgment for a nation that claims to champion liberty and justice for everyone.

[2]

WE THE PEOPLE VS. CONGRESS

BEFORE THERE WERE PRESIDENTS, THERE was a Congress. It had been established by the Constitution as the legislative branch of the federal government, with the purpose of drafting laws that all states were required to comply with. Although Congress continues to be central to American democracy, there has never been a Congress, in history, that has been less productive than the one we have right now.

Let's explore how we have arrived at this point.

Throughout its almost 250-year existence, Congress has fought several battles over the legislation it approves. It is the most significant branch since it represents, "We The People." Congress was created to enact new laws and to be equitable to all states. It is divided into two chambers, the House and Senate. Both chambers must agree on legislation before it becomes law, demonstrating their bipartisan role in governance.

Indeed, statistical data indicates that Congress's productivity, as measured by the number of laws enacted, has declined since 2008. The Congressional Research Service reports that recent Congresses have enacted a lower number of public legislation than historical averages. The 112th Congress (2011-2012) enacted just 283 public legislations, the lowest total since the commencement of record-keeping in 1947. Likewise, the 113th Congress (2013-2014) enacted 296 legislations, marking another record-low total.

The passage of fewer laws does not always indicate ineffectiveness; nonetheless, many enacted legislations were either non-controversial or symbolic, exerting minimal influence on significant national matters such as healthcare, immigration, or infrastructure. The 21st Century Cures Act, enacted in 2016 to accelerate medication approvals, was among the limited significant bipartisan legislative efforts; yet, it failed to tackle more extensive systemic issues.

Since 2008, after the election of an African American man to the highest position in the land, as President of the United States, also known as Commander in Chief, Congress has been under fire for refusing to address important national concerns. This perception is fueled by increased party polarization, legislative gridlock, and a significant decline in passing major legislation. The events subsequent to this administration, notably the attempt to repeal the Affordable Care Act, the controversial 2020 presidential election, and the aftermath of the attack on the Capital, signaled the beginning of a century marked by profound polarization in politics and a battle for bipartisan collaboration.

As a result of partisanship, Congress has often been unable to achieve an agreement on critical topics like healthcare reform, immigration, infrastructure, and gun control. The frequency of government shutdowns highlights this pattern, exposing a legislative body that fails to meet its basic obligations, which are fulfilling the needs of "We The People." Furthermore, Congress continues to put its own interests, party allegiance, and the demands of special interest groups ahead of what's best for, yet again, "We The People." This has been demonstrated by its failure to enact important laws despite widespread popular support for reforms.

The growing importance of money in politics has contributed to the notion that members are more concerned with self-preservation and political gain than with serving, the citizens of this nation. Executive orders have been forced since the Obama Administration, underscoring Congress' weakened role in government. Overall, the panorama of American politics depicts a Congress that often finds itself confined by division, resulting in broad public distrust and resentment towards Congress's ability to effectively serve the people in the greatest country in the world.

Following an election, the party that wins a majority of seats in each chamber can confidently call checkmate. Members of the minority party are frequently ineffective as a result. The majority party in the House of Representatives selects the Speaker, which is Congress's most powerful member. In 2007, California's Nancy Pelosi made history as the first female Speaker of the House. In the Senate, the party that has obtained the majority selects the Senate majority leader. This, too, is a powerful position. However, power was null and void for the upcoming Congress, because there was a split in the House and the Senate. This caused a political circus in Congress.

In 2009–2010, for example, Republicans came together to oppose the Affordable Care Act (ACA) primarily to deny the Obama administration a legislative win, rather than on the basis of the merits of healthcare reform in general. In spite of significant popular desire for healthcare reform, the partisan conflict culminated in a deeply divisive statute that was enacted without bipartisan endorsement. This conduct has recurred in later administrations, with both parties constantly prioritizing political considerations over the greater public interest, making Congress a political jungle. Seemingly, in today's Congress, the only way to accomplish its objectives occurs when the president belongs to the same political party that holds a majority in both the House and the Senate.

The Republican-dominated Congress, in 2017, prioritized the repeal of the Affordable Care Act(ACA) rather than improving the healthcare system in a way that addressed the concerns of a majority of Americans. Attempts to rescind the ACA concluded in many unsuccessful votes, including the notable "skinny repeal" vote, which narrowly failed in the Senate following considerable public opposition. Although a significant segment of the population opposed the repeal of the ACA, political interests prevailed in the discourse.

Congress has also failed to move the needle to address critical national issues, leaving many problems unresolved for years. One example is immigration reform. Despite multiple attempts, Congress has been unable to pass comprehensive immigration legislation, even as the issue has become increasingly urgent. The 2013 bipartisan immigration bill, which included a pathway to citizenship for undocumented immigrants and stronger border security measures, passed the Senate but was never brought to a vote in the House due to partisan infighting. The failure to act on immigration has led to continued uncertainty for millions of undocumented immigrants, as well as a broken immigration system that both parties acknowledge needs reform.

After a real estate mogul and reality-TV celebrity, campaigned and won the Republican presidential nomination, one of whom, never worked in a government office before, but that was precisely what his supporters wanted. He would become the one to tap into their prejudices and worst fears. The 45th would be quick to spread lies about opponents and eager to employ dirty techniques to gain his base's support and loyalty. In 2017, Republicans held a majority in both chambers of Congress. They enacted a large tax reduction that mostly benefitted the wealthy and tried to gain funding to curtail immigration regulations. A significant apprehension in Congress has been the escalating partisan gridlock, characterized by political parties prioritizing obstruction over the enactment of legislation that benefits the citizens of the country.

Also, under this administration, party allegiance frequently took precedence over tackling urgent national concerns. Despite widespread enthusiasm for immigration reform, Congress has consistently failed to achieve a bipartisan solution to issues such as Deferred Action for Childhood Arrivals (DACA). The matter was frequently used as a political instrument, with both parties aligning themselves to gain support from their constituents instead of pursuing a holistic resolution. Gun control laws are another example.

Despite several mass shootings and substantial popular endorsement for more stringent gun regulations, Congress has been

unable to enact significant gun control legislation.

Proposals for enhanced background
checks, prohibitions on assault weapons, and
other changes have consistently been ob-
structed, mostly owing to the influence of
special interest organizations such as the National Rifle Association (NRA) and apprehension of electoral repercussions in
elections.

This delay has faced extensive criticism
for Congress preferring its affiliations with
influential lobbying entities and its electoral
prospects over the safety of the country's
children and adults. The confirmation of
Supreme Court justices during this time also
indicated Congress's emphasis on party ad-
vantages. The Senate Republicans' refusal to
vote on President Obama's nominee, Mer-
rick Garland, in 2016, coupled with the expedited confirmation of Amy Coney Barrett
shortly before the 2020 election, exemplified
Congress's growing tendency to prioritize

political gain over institutional norms and the public's long-term interests.

The 45th sought to erect a wall along the Mexican border to keep unauthorized immigrants out. Despite having a majority in both chambers, Congress did not approve all of the funding requested by the 45th. Nonetheless, the Senate ensured that hundreds of the 45th's judicial nominations were elected. All of which are conservative in their political views. Because of his popularity among his constituents, Congress became extremely loyal to the 45th. He was even able to gain party allegiance in his Congress, which aided him in carrying out lies to conceal his crimes, 34 of which he has been convicted. So, how can the 45th run in the 2024 presidential election? That's covered in a later chapter.

As we've learned from the past, when one party controls the House and the other controls the Senate, the government can become gridlocked. Following the 2018 Congressional elections, for example, Democrats took control of the House. Nancy Pelosi was re-elected Speaker. However, Republicans retained control of the Senate. The two parties had extremely different opinions about what types of laws should be enacted. The Senate majority leader at the time was Republican Mitch McConnell, also known as the "Grim Reaper" of Kentucky. He was well known for being non-compliant with House-sponsored Senate bills. He refused to even read the bills, let alone vote on them. Perhaps notes were taken on the 45th's administration? Wait, silly me, he was a part of the administration.

While the president has the power to veto a measure, a two-thirds vote in each chamber can overturn it.

Additionally, there is a pocket veto. This occurs when the president does not sign or veto (reject) a law. He waits until Congress adjourns and the bill dies. For example, the 45th President oversaw the longest shutdown in US history, which lasted 35 days (December 22, 2018 - January 25, 2019). The 45th and Congress disagreed on financing for a border wall along the United States-Mexico border. The 45th wanted $5.7 billion for the wall, but Democrats in Congress blocked the financing. The shutdown ended when the 45th agreed to temporarily reopen the government without getting financing for the wall, however, he later proclaimed a national emergency to reroute funds for its construction, which never took place.

There were bipartisan initiatives to improve border security and border patrol resources. However, the 45th frequently rejected similar measures if they did not line with his wider immigration agenda, particularly if they did not include sufficient funds for the border wall or had provisions for DACA individuals that did not meet his requirements. In February 2018, the Senate debated several immigration measures, one of which was a bipartisan package that contained $25 billion for border security (including the wall) in return for a road to citizenship for DACA recipients. The 45th voted against this measure because he felt it did not go far enough in addressing other immigration concerns, such as banning chain migration and the diversity visa lottery. As a result, it did not pass, despite the fact that bipartisan agreements were reached that contained Border Patrol elements.

Unfortunately, the kind of bipartisanship observed during the Watergate affair is inconceivable in today's Congress. However, despite rising division, Congress has seen times of remarkable bipartisanship since Watergate. Some significant instances are

1. Reagan's tax revisions (1986). Democrats and Republicans

collaborated to streamline the
tax law.

2. Civil Rights Restoration Act,
   1988. Overriding a presidential
   veto, Congress approved this bill,
   which ensures wider rights.

3. The Americans with Disabilities
   Act of 1990. Passed with wide
   bipartisan support to protect
   persons with disabilities.

4. The Affordable Care Act
   amendments (2010) and the
   COVID-19 stimulus packages
   (2020). Both witnessed
   collaborations, however
   controversial.

Although Congress has been sharply split along party lines in the last 25 years, maybe more than at any point since the years leading up to the Civil War. Today, even friendships between party leaders are uncommon. Control of Congress has passed from Democrats to Republicans and back multiple times, making it increasingly difficult for Congress to approve legislation. Or legislation would be passed by one Congress and then repealed by a subsequent Congress.

Congress functions similarly to a chess game, characterized by strategic maneuvers, deliberate choices, and a nuanced equilibrium of authority. Both need strategic foresight, navigation of challenges, and the pursuit of success—whether by enacting laws or checkmating the adversary's ruler. Nonetheless, akin to chess, the efficacy of Congress hinges on the expertise, motives, and collaboration of the participants engaged. The juxtaposition between Congress and chess underscores the strengths and shortcomings of the legislative institution.

In chess, the initial moves are essential for establishing a robust foundation, similar to how Congress must start each session with crucial legislative goals. At its optimal state,

Congress can resemble a meticulously prepared chess opening, with all pieces (representatives and senators) carefully positioned for collaboration. Bipartisan collaboration on matters such as national security or infrastructure may result in prompt, efficient legislation that serves the interests of the whole nation. When Congress concentrates on common objectives, such as economic recovery or disaster relief, it may effectively enact legislation that benefits millions of Americans, akin to a chess player adeptly maneuvering their pieces to dominate the board.

But like chess, Congress may easily devolve into dysfunction if the first moves are made badly. When partisan deadlock ensues early in a session, advancing legislation becomes challenging, as both factions prioritize opposing one another above facilitating progress. Similar to a chess player who adopts a purely defensive strategy, Congress may find itself in a condition of stagnation, when no significant progress is made due to one faction's preoccupation with countering the other's initiatives.

In chess, the midgame is characterized by predominant tactical maneuvers, as pieces align for critical engagement. This phase in Congress signifies the discussion and committee efforts involved in formulating legislation and modifications. The midgame highlights the positive attributes of Congress, as legislators engage in discussion, deliberation, and compromise to produce legislation that tackles intricate challenges. Similar to chess, where participants must predict their adversary's actions and modify their tactics, proficient members of Congress attentively weigh diverse perspectives, evaluate potential repercussions, and pursue consensus to advance the nation.

Regrettably, here is where the worst aspects of Congress become apparent. Similar to a chess player who becomes excessively cautious or aims for a draw rather than a victory, Congress frequently enters a pattern of evading decisive actions. Political self-interest may prevail, as legislators prioritize re-election or party allegiance above addressing substantive issues. This is seen in instances where Congress refrains from addressing contentious matters such as immigration reform or healthcare, as doing so may jeopardize political backing. Rather than taking decisive action, Congress frequently opts for interim measures, such as short-term budget resolutions, which just postpone essential answers and indicate a deficiency in long-term foresight.

The endgame in chess is the phase where the objective—checkmate—is imminent. In Congress, the endgame signifies the last phases of legislation, during which a bill requires ratification from both chambers and must be enacted into law. When Congress operates well, the conclusion may be as definitive and skillfully accomplished as a brilliant checkmate. The expedited enactment of COVID-19 relief legislation in 2020 demonstrated Congress's capacity to respond promptly during emergencies, delivering essential support to distressed individuals and enterprises.

Nonetheless, the adverse aspects of Congress's conclusion are equally evident. Similar to a chess player who fails to secure a winning position, Congress might stumble in the concluding phase. Legislative achievements are frequently compromised by last-minute political tactics, filibusters, or threats of veto. This may lead to ineffective legislation that does not tackle the core issue, or, in certain instances, the absence of any legislation altogether. The recent history of government shutdowns and debt limit crises underscores Congress's challenges in effectively resolving critical issues, resulting in national instability.

[3]

WE THE PEOPLE VS. UNFAIR LAWS

"For I was hungry and you gave me something to eat, I was thirsty and you gave me something to drink, I was a stranger and you invited me in, I needed clothes and you clothed me, I was sick and you looked after me, I was in prison and you came to visit me. Then the righteous will answer him, Lord when did we see you hungry and feed you, or thirsty and give you something to drink? When did we see you a stranger and invite you in, or needing clothes and clothe you? When did we see you sick or in prison and go visit you? The King will reply, Truly I tell you, whatever you did for one of the least of these brothers and sisters of mine, you did for me."

- MATTHEW 25:35-40 (NIV)

THESE VERSES CONVEY SPIRITUAL AND moral qualities like love, compassion, and service to others. Jesus teaches us that when we help those in need, we are serving Him directly. He goes on to clarify that when we are kind and compassionate toward others, we are also kind and compassionate towards Him. Jesus makes it clear that helping those in need is a reflection of true righteousness. One of His commands to us is to serve with selflessness.

For instance, Jesus says in Matthew 20:28 (NIV),

"Just as the Son of Man did not come to be served, but to serve, and to give His life as a ransom for many."

He also says,

"Do nothing out of selfish ambition or vain conceit. Rather, in humility, value others above yourselves, not looking to your own interest but each of you to the interests of the others,"

- PHILIPPIANS 2:3-4 (NIV)

This exposes our true relationship with God. This is an expression of love for both God and neighbor.

A corrupt leader serves neither Christ nor the country's citizens. Unjust legislation does not represent Christ's righteousness. They are in grave contradiction to both God's Life and God's Word. Committing to follow Christ should lead your actions and moral decisions, even if it means standing up to injustice and political resistance. True patriotism doesn't imply having a blind allegiance to injustice, but rather governing for the greater good of "We The People."

A true patriot, in leadership positions or not, cares about their country's moral integrity, recognizing that justice is essential to the country's strength and future. Questioning and condemning unjust actions, policies, and laws is loving yourself, your neighbor, and your country. There is no morality in intentional disinformation.

Serving "For the People" should never be for personal wealth or glory. Serving "For the People," should not imply authoritarianism or dictatorship. Neither humility nor integrity is preferable in isolation. They both play critical roles in leadership and government. Together, they form a well-rounded and effective leader.

Both are critical and serve as important reminders to society's governing institutions that they are in positions of leadership "By The People." The first line of the Constitution's preamble "We the people, for the people, by the people" captures the essence of democracy. The people wield power, the government exists to serve them, and the people engage in the processes that define the nation. Leadership represents the interest of ALL its citizens.

The more laws change, the more they remain the same.

Hence the evolution of the United States Constitution and its twenty-seven amendments. Although it has evolved over time to address many of its flaws, its original form, presented both true and false statements about freedom and inclusiveness.

Making the document extremely flawed. For example, legalizing slavery, excluding the Bill of Rights, and limiting voting rights to only white male property owners. While this supreme law of the United States laid the foundation for a democratic government, its original form has been the cause of continued systemic issues affecting ethnic minority groups today.

It is said, and true, that the end of an era marks the beginning of a new one. Reflecting the natural swing of change from past to future. Perhaps a replica of a pendulum-style swing. Typically, under the influence of gravity, a pendulum swings back and forth in a regular and predictable pattern. The back-and-forth motion is considered one full swing. The time it takes for that single swing to occur is referred to as its period, and it is influenced by the length of the pendulum and the acceleration due to gravity. However, the motion of the pendulum can become unpredictable under certain conditions.

As an example, in terms of the United States' formation, the pendulum swung from evil to evil. This became a repetitive reality for the Native and African American minority groups. One group was forced to be removed while the other was forced to be admitted. Both were forced under duress, to put it mildly. Colonialism, slavery, segregation, and unjust laws are deep-rooted legal cornerstones that have helped shape the United States of America into what we know today. These policies and institutions present a framework for understanding the history and development of the country as they relate to racism and discrimination. These governmental directives were established for the benefit of White American settlers.

Colonialism is the pendulum's initial swing. It's the foundation for white supremacy, exploitation, and oppression. Although its concept is no longer applicable, manifest destiny was a perverted ideal created by White American settlers under the guise of divine order with a divine right to take and conquer the American continent. This ideology shaped the geographic and political landscape of the United States. It served as a reason for displacing Native Americans, reinforcing white supremacy, and expanding westward. White supremacists morally justified their actions because they believed they were superior. Encouraging more settlers to relocate west in pursuit of land ownership and opportunity.

For thousands of years before European colonialism, Native Americans inhabited North America. The 'Trail of Tears' and the 'Indian Removal Act' of 1830 are historical accounts of the forced exodus of Native Americans from their homelands. The exodus was the direct result of federal authority and policies enacted under then-president Andrew Jackson.

Andrew Jackson, the 7th president of the United States, who served from 1829 to 1837, ideologies of governing was of limited government and upholding states' rights. He was for white supremacy. Therefore, he was pro-slavery. The goal of the forced exodus was to remove Native Americans and their tribes from their ancestral lands to make way for white settlers. In order to swap Native American lands in the southeast for lands west of the Mississippi River, President Jackson gave the federal government permission to negotiate treaties. These treaties were to define boundaries of Native American lands from new European settled lands and to compensate Native Americans for simply taking their lands.

The betrayal with these treaties, is that they were never honored, tracing back to the flawed inclusiveness of the Constitution.

President Jackson used military force to remove the Native Americans. The Cherokee, Choctaw, Chickasaw, Creek, and Seminole Indian tribes were among those forced to relocate. They were removed from the southern states of Georgia, Alabama, Mississippi, and Florida to what is known as Oklahoma Reservation Territory or Indian Territory. From the early 1800s to the late nineteenth century, this land was regarded as a separate entity from the United States due to the ceding of territory in the east.

Nonetheless, the Oklahoma Land Rush of 1889 disrupted the inhabitation of this territory by making substantial portions of this land available to white settlers, when it had previously been pledged only to Native Americans. This moment in time marks the end of the "Indian Territory" and the beginning of a merged state with white settlers, which significantly weakened the fabric of the Indian Territory and culture. The move showed a clear disregard and lack of respect for the sovereignty and rights of Native Americans.

Inclusiveness lost its way. However, in

the Supreme Court ruling, of McGirt v. Oklahoma (2020), Native Americans retained ownership of their property in Oklahoma.

Not so much as the agreement of Fort Laramie. The United States promised in this 1868 treaty to reserve the Great Sioux Reservation, which includes the Black Hills, for the sole and continuous use and possession of the Lakota Nation. However, the finding of gold in the area, caused the United States to want to acquire back the Black Hills. Of course, the Lakota turned down the offer, sparking the Black Hills War (1876-1877). Despite a temporary victory at the Battle of Little Bighorn for the Native Americans, the United States ultimately forced them to give up their land.

Through further bullying and betrayal, Congress reversed the original deal and passed legislation to recapture the Black Hills. In 1923, the Lakota Nation filed a lawsuit. _Sixty_ years later, the Supreme Court ruled that the annulment constituted a 'take' under the Fifth Amendment and that the tribe was entitled to compensation. The offer was declined.

Lakota is demanding the restitution of the land. As of 2018, the amount owed is said to be around $1 billion dollars.

Today, Native Americans, are concentrated in certain areas of the United States as well as off-reservation in urban areas, reflecting both historical displacement and modern migration. "We The People, For The People, and By The People," seems to have lost its way.

The swing of the pendulum from colonialism to slavery did not alter the trajectory of African Americans. However, severe oppression had remained constant. Reflecting the control of white supremacy and deepening the injustices experienced by enslaved African Americans. It was a recurring cycle of racism and persecution. The legal systems were designed to maintain control over African Americans as property rather than citizens of the United States. The Constitution implicitly denied citizenship to all African Americans, free or enslaved, hence the Dred Scott v. Sanford ruling in 1857 which exemplifies the Three-Fifths Compromise and the Fugitive Slave Clause.

The Three-Fifths Compromise was an agreement that stated that three-fifths of a state's enslaved population would be counted as part of its overall population when determining representation in the House of Representatives and for taxation purposes. It was established to settle a dispute between Northern and Southern states about how to count slaves when calculating a state's population for congressional representation. In contrast, the Fugitive Slave Clause granted the slave owner the authority to retrieve an enslaved individual who had fled to another state. Following that, the Fugitive Slave Act of 1850 required all states to seize and return slaves. This resulted in abolitionist resistance and a split between free and slave states, which contributed to the Civil War.

The pendulum then swings back towards freedom as abolitionist movements gain traction. Individuals and groups began to fight for freedom to escape the dehumanizing effects of slavery. The end of slavery symbolizes a major societal shift that was met with resistance and resentment which was preparing for the next swing. Despite achieving freedom, the pendulum swings to new challenges and unjust laws.

The liberation of slavery led to the pendulum's swing back toward oppression in the form of unfair laws, which were then utilized to impose racism, injustice, and discrimination through America's judicial system. Black Codes, for example, served as the precursor to Jim Crow laws. Influenced by the legality of racism, these regulations were enacted to restrict the civil rights of

African Americans and maintain systemic racism. Jim Crow laws and black codes were examples of structurally constructed discrimination. They threatened the rule of law, justice, and equality. This counter-swing reflects how societal structure can lead to discriminatory practices.

Black codes were created during the Reconstruction era following the Civil War to limit the civil rights of African Americans by dictating their places of employment and residence as well as their interactions with the criminal justice system. For example, there were limits on voting, serving on juries, and testifying against white individuals. Limiting their freedom of movement, compelling them to sign annual labor contracts, and imposing severe penalties for vagrancy or unemployment.

Jim Crow laws, imposed by local and state governments, institutionalized segregation and discrimination, requiring segregation in all aspects of African American everyday life, with the majority being enforced in the south of the United States. Jim Crow laws required African Americans and White Americans to have segregated access to schools, transportation, bathrooms, drinking fountains, and other public facilities. These facilities were unfair and inadequate for African Americans.

It was prohibited for African Americans to dine at the same hotels and restaurants as White Americans. African American children received unequal and segregated educational opportunities. African Americans were prevented from voting by a variety of tactics, including literacy exams and voting poll levies. Voting fees were added to poll taxes, and the literacy exam was arbitrarily and tediously administered. Jim Crow laws banned White and African Americans from marrying or engaging in any other type of partnership.

Due to redlining, these regulations also prevented African Americans from renting or purchasing homes in White communities, limiting them to low-wage labor-intensive jobs such as sharecropping, tenant farming, cooks, maids, and manual labor in construction, railroads, factories, and mining.

The swing toward the civil rights movement emerged as a response to the injustices of prior times. Activists began to protest and overturn these unfair laws, advocating for equality and justice. This phase focuses on the collective movement for civil rights and the call for systemic reform, with the ultimate goal of stabilizing the pendulum in a more just position.

God made all mankind in His likeness. The Bible teaches that every individual, regardless of race or ethnicity is created in his image. In the first book of the Holy Bible, Genesis 1:27 (NIV) says,

"So God created man in his own image, in the image of God created he him; male and female created he them."

This verse simply states that every person has intrinsic worth, and respect regardless of their racial background. Therefore, whatever is contrary to this is a lie.

Revelation 7:9 (NIV), further describes a great multitude from all nations, countries, tribes, peoples, and languages standing before God. The verse reads,

"After this, I looked, and there before me was a great multitude that no one could count, from every nation, tribe, people, and language, standing before the throne and before the Lamb. They were holding palm branches in their hands."

The white robes portray a standing of righteousness who are praising God for their salvation. Therefore, racial superiority is a lie and human variation does not imply a hierarchy of worth or ability.

The atmosphere had begun to shift once again. This time, however, there was a sweet aroma in the air. The pendulum had begun to swing towards liberty and change. The Civil War (1861-1865) represented a swing towards justice, as it abolished slavery with the Emancipation Proclamation (1863) and later the 13th Amendment (1865). This era was characterized by a desire to rebuild the nation and establish rights for newly emancipated African Americans. This swing concluded with the Reconstruction Act of 1867, which sought to reconstruct the South by granting emancipated slaves basic human rights and political involvement. This period also saw the passage of amendments and reforms aimed at advancing equality, such as the 13th and 14th amendments abolishing slavery, ensuring due process and equal protection of the laws, and finally ensuring voting rights for African Americans were implemented.

"For every action, there is an equal and opposite reaction." After Reconstruction, the pendulum swung back toward oppression. Although they experienced a brief period of political and social advancement, resulting in the appointment of African Americans to public office. The gains were systematically undermined once again by the Black Codes and Jim Crow laws and the newly formed KU KLUX KLAN. They once again, severely restricted African American civil rights. On Christmas Eve in 1865, a group of determined southern racist Confederate veterans assembled in Pulaski, Tennessee, to organize the Ku Klux Klan. They were determined to reverse the federal government's progressive Reconstruction policies. They did not support policies that increased the rights of African Americans. They eventually grew to be the largest domestic terrorist organization in the United States.

The combination of new southern Jim Crow legislation co-signed by the Supreme Court and the KKK's violent force harmed the achievements gained soon after the Civil War ended. Even when African American communities thrived economically and politically, white supremacist terrorists would raid or assault entire towns and burn them down.

Notable examples are Rosewood, Florida, Tulsa, Oklahoma, known as "Black Wall Street," and Forsyth County, Georgia. In Forsyth County, Georgia, an entire population of a flourishing agricultural African American town who owned their land was terrorized into fleeing out of the county or risking death. Later the town would be covered by a massive man-made body of water known as Lake Lanier.

Economically, African Americans were locked in cycles of brutal manual labor with poor wages, leaving them in a position of economic servitude despite their legal liberty. Socially, they confront segregation, brutality, and disenfranchisement, resulting in pervasive social and economic subjugation. The pendulum here represents the "rollback of progress," in which freedom was limited and equality denied.

Furthermore, at the turn of the century, a group known as the Daughters of the Confederacy was formed. These affluent wives and daughters of elderly and former Confederate soldiers utilized their wealth to establish long-term, racist strongholds throughout the southern states. In the South, Confederate daughters wielded immense power. By vetting, screening, and certifying every book used by Southern schools and libraries, they took over the region's educational system and shaped the narrative of how history was taught, ensuring that the content romanticized the institution of slavery. In addition, they would ensure that the horrors of Rosewood, Florida, Tulsa, Oklahoma, and Forsyth

County would not have a place in their history.

They were also in charge of erecting monuments and statues of Confederate soldiers in nearly every Southern town square. Even though the Civil War was lost, the Daughters of the Confederacy worked to ensure that White supremacy's legacy endured. The discriminatory system in America was reintroduced with the Supreme Court's endorsement of "Separate but Equal" legislation and bigoted control over the educational system. This control would extend decades, even into the early 1980s in states such as Florida. So it's not surprising that just a few years later, we'd witness a return of this push for control over the school system, this time in the shape of anti-critical race theory rhetoric.

As previously stated, Critical Race Theory is a concept that seeks to comprehend the Constitution and laws by studying their history and evolution. Again, we cannot grasp the current state of race and discrimination until we have a thorough understanding of its history and growth. Our politicians, educational systems, and white supremacists, on the other hand, used the word to agitate Americans and parents of elementary school pupils who are uneasy with facts.

They invented this fake narrative in order to erase the history of African Americans from the educational system.

This is the latest attempt at rewriting history. Hidden beneath the guise of preventing hatred, these organizations are ultimately more interested in maintaining white supremacy than in promoting equality for all people and safeguarding the truth. This movement, led by groups such as Moms for Liberty, is simply a rebranding of the same old tradition. The purpose is to erase the facts of our history and whitewash information about our country's past in order to romanticize white supremacy's destruction in the South.

However, the pendulum swings back toward the emergence of the civil rights movement. African Americans and their allies like Rosa Parks and Dr. Martin Luther King fought against racial segregation, disenfranchisement, and economic inequality. This period marked a significant push against the repressive systems of Black Codes, Jim Crow, and the KU KLUX KLAN, with landmark events like the Montgomery Bus Boycott (1955-1956) and March on Washington (1963), swinging the pendulum back toward a renewed demand for civil rights.

The forward swing of the Civil Rights Movement ended with the passing of historic legislation. The Civil Rights Act of 1964 prohibited racial discrimination in public places, employment, and education while the Voting Rights Act of 1965 aimed to legally preserve and protect African American voting rights. These statutes were a high point of progress, representing the pendulum swinging toward greater equality and justice under the law. It demonstrated official, legal acknowledgment of African Americans' long-fought-battle for equal rights. However, the pendulum movement did not end there; even after these legal achievements, the fight for complete equality and justice continues.

We see differences in sentencing based on factors unrelated to crime, such as race and income. This defies the foundational ideals of justice. These principles are fairness (ensuring that all citizens are treated equally and without bias), equality (ensuring that all citizens have the same rights and opportunities), impartiality (ensuring that all decisions are based on objective criteria), accountability (ensuring that all citizens are held accountable for their actions and decisions), and due process (ensuring that all citizens receive a fair procedure). These principles were established to ensure that the American judicial system functions with integrity and fairness.

However, without wavering into the 21st century, white supremacy continues to permeate American society. We are presently experiencing contradictions in these foundational ideals and how the Constitution is interpreted and enforced. Our society is witnessing the corruption in our government and criminal justice system. Members of our judicial and governmental institutions appear to have had their backbones ripped out and thrown to the ground by the Antichrist. How is it legal for presidents to appoint judges who have conservative interpretations of the Constitution and are likely to oppose equal justice and opportunity under our laws?

So how does a "high crime" such as the act of domestic terrorism go unchecked? How does a thirty-four-time convicted felon run for the highest office in the land when tied to espionage and treason? How does one who is a thirty-four-time criminal who has been convicted of sexual assault become the Republican party's presidential candidate? Are we witnessing the new version of Eugene V. Debs, who ran for President while serving a prison sentence for his anti-war activism in 1920? The stark difference here is that he was promoting peace, whereas, the imposter is asserting a complete judicial and governmental takeover. Where is the integrity of the party?

In fact, where is the integrity of the judicial system? Unfortunately, American history provides a clear and unequivocal explanation. It's the same unilateral racial tradition of privilege played out with new characters.

With the expansion of minority groups, as well as other variables such as birth rates, immigration, and interracial marriages, the U.S. Population is increasing its diversity. Perhaps Jim Crow is turning over in 'its' abstract grave, or, more concretely, bigoted White American Thomas Dartmouth Rice, who conceived and portrayed the racial caricature, is turning over in his.

Racial minority populations in America make up a lower percentage of the population than that of White Americans. While White Americans roughly account for 61.6% of the nation, they hold less than 1% of the world's population. If we consider people of European descent, their percentage 'might' climb from 1% to 10-12%.

The population percentages of the following racial minority groups are as follows: Latinos 19%, African Americans 14%, Multiracial group "which is the fastest growing group in the country" is currently at 10%, Asian Americans 7%, Middle Eastern and North African Americans 3%, Native Americans 2%, and Native Hawaiian and Pacific Islander Americans 1%, all of which experienced institutional racism, injustice, and discrimination. The American social system is still wrecked with racist laws and regulations that fail to provide equal protection, equal opportunity, and equal civil advancement.

The US Census Bureau predicts that by 2045, White Americans will no longer constitute the majority of the population, accounting for less than half of the total. This means that the United States will become a "majority-minority" nation by 2045. In terms of time, twenty-one years does not seem very long.

[4]
WE THE PEOPLE VS THE ANTICHRIST

THE UNITED STATES OF AMERICA WAS not founded as a Christian nation. The Founding Fathers, a diverse group of men, with varying views on government and religion were deliberate with their secular underpinnings of the Constitution. Although they encapsulated a mixture of beliefs such as Christianity, Deism, Episcopalian, and Unitarian, they had no intention of establishing the country as a Christian nation. Perhaps their different religious beliefs are the cause of the secular Republic framework that advocates for the separation of church and state. In fact, "We The People, For The People, and By The People," does not constitute a religious belief. It does, however, establish the foundation for the principle of self-government. This further means, that the government is empowered by its citizens, who hold the power to elect their officials of representation.

Although Christianity was not its foundation, the United States was neither built on the idea of authoritarianism nor dictatorship.

The foundation of the United States of America has never underscored the sovereignty of "The Father, The Son, and the Holy Spirit." Therefore, Christianity was not of central importance to the Founders more than setting a foundation for the democratic governance to represent and serve the citizens through the popular sovereignty of, "We The People, For The People, and By The People." Perhaps we are confused in our thinking that the country has a religious Christian heritage because of the "Star Spangled Banner."

For example, it says, "I pledge allegiance to the flag, of the United States of America, and to the Republic for which it stands, one Nation under God, indivisible, with liberty and justice for all." In its original form, it did not include the controversial mentioning of "one Nation under God," which was included to distinguish itself from atheist nations. Hence, the reason for the ongoing controversy includes the idea that the state has merged with the church. Be it as it may, the pledge is to the flag and the nation, and not to any specific religion or God. Even though Christian Nationalists seem to think so.

Christian nationalism is a cultural and political ideology that merges Christian identity with national identity. "They believe that either the founding of the U.S. was _heavily influenced_ by Christianity and that the Founding Fathers _intended_ for the country to reflect Christian values in its governance." Conclusively, the evidence of facts and actions of the United States legal and judicial systems throughout history, utterly disputes this belief as inaccurate. The Founding Fathers who were Christians, arguably were cultural Christians. Meaning they identified with Christian traditions, values, or practices, rather than having a deeper spiritual conviction or reverence of God.

Cultural Christians do not actively attend church; however, you will see them in church for specific occasions like Easter Sunday. They do not practice their faith by reading or studying the Bible. They even hold theological beliefs by understanding morality but do the opposite of its principles. Their connection to Christ is about cultural identity rather than a spiritual relationship. God calls these Christians "lukewarm." This is a Christian who exhibits a lack of fervor, spiritual growth, and faith. Their influence is worldly and are comfortable with sin. Revelation 3:15-16 (NIV), says,

> "I know your deeds, that you are neither cold nor hot. I wish you were either one or the other! So, because you are lukewarm, neither hot nor cold, I am about to spit you out of my mouth."

Significantly in saying, this type of Christian is worthless.

Although Christianity is the dominant religion in the United States (approximately 65-70% of the population), secularism is the supporting foundation of the supreme law of the country. It gives the right to an individual to practice any religion or simply no religion at all. Hence, have left the door open for the anti-Christ to wield its dark and evil spirit through the nation.

"For our struggle is not against flesh and blood, but against the rulers, against the authorities, against the powers of this dark world and against the spiritual forces of evil in the heavenly realms"

- EPHESIANS 6:12 (NIV)

This verse emphasizes that Christians' true battle is not against other human beings but against spiritual evil. Like demonic forces that hold influence of power in the spiritual realm. These powers influence the world and are responsible for the moral and spiritual darkness we see in our society.

Some people are even possessed by demons. They are committed to doing evil and are involved in various occult and cult practices. Both vary in meaning and practice. The occult is about having "secret" knowledge connected to the supernatural. Examples of the practice are astrology, tarot, alchemy, and witchcraft. A cult, by contrast, centers around a group's devotion to a leader or belief system, often demanding loyalty and control over its members. While both practices are manipulative and harmful, we will focus on the cult practice later in this chapter.

Evil manifests itself in various forms. Its spiritual characteristics influence lies, ill-gotten power and success, immorality, destruction, chaos, racism, deception, political manipulation, injustice, political corruption, pride, violence, narcissism, and lawlessness.

The Bible says in Daniel 8:25 (KJV)

"And through his policy also he shall cause craft to prosper in his hand, and he shall magnify himself in his heart, and by peace shall destroy many: he shall also stand up against the Prince of princes, but he shall be broken without hand."

The New International Version of this same verse says,

> "He will cause deceit to prosper, and he will consider himself superior.
> When they feel secure, he will destroy many and take his stand against the Prince of princes. Yet he will be destroyed, but not by human power."

Although this verse is referencing the antichrist during the Tribulation period, God is allowing, "We The People" to have a precursor of what it will look like in the future during the actual period. It will, however, be gravely worse. Further, in this verse, "We The People," also bear witness concerning the ruler's cunning manipulations but ultimate downfall. In dissecting this verse, it is easy to see that the resemblance of the antichrist is already here. The Bible says, in 1 John 4:1-3 (KJV),

"Beloved, believe not every spirit, but try the spirits whether they are of God: because many false prophets are gone out into the world. Hereby know ye the Spirit of God: Every spirit that confesses that Jesus Christ has come in the flesh is of God: And every spirit that confesses not that Jesus Christ has come in the flesh is not of God: and this is that spirit of the antichrist, whereof ye have heard that it should come; and even now already is it in the world."

Perhaps this is relevant today of a man standing on the sidewalk with the Bible upside down in one hand while manipulating the nation with the other. Revealing his arrogance and haughty spirit. But as God reveals to us in the Bible, pride goes before destruction.

The essence of the antichrist is deceit. His plans are so well thought out, that he executes them with such skill and dexterity; often succeeding in getting people to believe him through disinformation and misinformation. Both of these purposefully manipulate, mislead, and influence public opinions and behaviors. It is essential to understand that before beholding the ultimate power of the free world, billionaire status, and influence was and is his charisma.

Being unchecked and untouched is his belief system. Manipulation and deception are indoctrinated through repetitive cult rhetoric of "us versus them" that harnesses his control over his followers' thought processes and behaviors. Fear-mongering, exploitation, and white supremacy are his characteristics. Over time, in fact, for the past 16 years, he has been able to deepen his followers' loyalty, making it seemingly impossible for them to question his lies. Of which, a cult ensues.

For example, in the last four years, there have been significant incidents of political violence such as The Michigan Governor Kidnapping Plot (2020); Threats and Violence Against Election Officials (2020); Protests and Riots after George Floyd's execution (2020); the Assault on Paul Pelosi (2022); and the most significant of them all, the violent and deadly January 6th U.S. Capital Attack on American Democracy (2021). The strategic objectives of these significant incidents aimed to undermine trust in American democracy and advance white supremacy by all means necessary.

The attack was a result of the then president's commission to supporters to disrupt the 2020 election certification results. The attacks were the result of the insidious rhetoric from a self-serving individual saying, "You'll never take back our country with weakness, you have to show strength and you have to be strong," even further saying, "I'll be there with you." It's pure political corruption and political manipulation when the executive branch attempts to completely undermine the democratic process. However,

> "O generation of vipers, how can ye, being evil, speak good things? For out of the abundance of the heart the mouth speaks,"
>
> — MATTHEW 12:34

Therefore, what one says is often a reflection of their true character, and astroturfing any idea is creating a fabricated consensus. It is our duty as "We The People" to outsmart the devil.

Christians should be careful to obey the Word of God to the best of his ability.

How does a nation claim Christian values when it is not based upon the Grace of God? Lies and manipulation have misled the public into believing in a false narrative, causing erosion within American democracy. Disinformation of a stolen election through widespread voter fraud is intentional and dangerous. It is also intentional and dangerous to incite mobsters to storm the U.S. Capital, at a morning rally just south of the White House, on the exact day Congress was meeting to certify the election results. Seven lives were lost that day: four supporters of the then-president and three capital police officers (two of whom died by suicide).

Some of the mobsters even called for the killing of then-Vice President Mike Pence via "hanging" because of his role in certifying the electoral college results. Nancy Pelosi, the Speaker of the House at the time, wasn't safe either. "Where's Nancy?" was being chanted as a few mobsters rifled through the Capital building looking for her. The evidence of this intent was manifested in the form of two fully constructed and functioning gallows that were stationed outside the capital building that very day. I regard this singular attack on the U.S. Capital as the most significant attack on American democracy in modern history.

The collective cause of these incidents is the emergence of unchecked political manipulation driven by lies and the unwillingness of a peaceful transfer of political power, which is the cornerstone of the U.S. political system.

Continuous polarization, misinformation, extremism, and the inciting rhetoric of an insurrection are a clear threat to the rule of law. Leading people astray, turning them away from the truth, and bringing destruction and chaos are deceptive qualities of the antichrist. The Bible clearly tells us to,

> "Let no man deceive you by any means: for that day shall not come, except there come a falling away first, and that man of sin be revealed, the son of perdition,"

> — 2 THESSALONIANS 2:3

An essential component of party conventions since 1972 has been the delegate roll call vote. Previously, party leaders would secretly meet in "smoke-filled rooms" to select their choice. These deals, not having been made in public, were perceived as components of the "old boss system," an undemocratic process. Perhaps today, that same process would look like a private telephone conversation with the Georgia Secretary of State, to find 11,780 votes to overturn the 2020 presidential election results. The then-incumbent tried to convince state officials to alter certified election results.

The United States' "checks and balances" system is intended to prevent the three branches of government from abusing their power. Maintaining political governance is the responsibility of every branch. The commander in chief, also referred to as the head of state, is the leader of the free world, but he or she is not allowed to enact laws that restrict the ability of any one voter.

The president cannot amend the constitution, remove senators or representatives, eliminate the Department of Education, FEMA, or EPA, or choose how to use tax revenue by bypassing Congress. "We The People, For The People, and By The People," describes the democratic system in the United States. The root of the government's authority and power is the people it serves.

Evil deceptively presents itself as an agent of good while holding the Bible upside down in one hand and undermining the process of an election in the other. Luke 6:46 quotes God as saying, "And why call ye me, Lord, Lord, and do not the things which I say?" In other words, why hold up the Bible when you don't even read it! The Bible warns us of being misled by appearances and the need for us to have discernment. The Apostle Paul warns us in 2 Corinthians 11:14 that

"Satan himself masquerades as an angel of light,"

implying that evil disguises itself as good. Propaganda is a tool used by dictators to control the narrative and manipulate public opinion. They possess an antichrist spirit that seeks to impose fear and intimidation along with threats of violence, as a way of preserving political authority and maintaining order.

The antichrist is deceptive and charismatic and is the ultimate adversary of good. He blurs the line between right and wrong, good and evil, fear and faith. God specifically says to believers,

"For God has not given us the spirit of fear; but of power, and of love, and of a sound mind"

- 2 TIMOTHY 1:7

God encourages believers to rely on faith to overcome fear and live with courage, love, and self-control. This is morality. This is righteousness. This is true power.

In this world, there are many spirits, but the Holy Spirit—the third member of the Holy Trinity—is the only one with ultimate authority. All Christians believe in the theology of the Holy Trinity, which holds that there is only one God who exists eternally in three distinct persons: God the Father, God the Son, and God the Holy Spirit (Matthew 28:19). The Triune God is one in essence but three in person, equal in nature and authority, independent of one another, intimately related, and is eternal love.

The antichrist spirit is the opposite of love. While it may masquerade behind a veil of love, the antichrist spirit is ultimately looking to unleash power, control, and fear.

Rather than emulating God, it attempts to imitate Him through power and authority. It uses deception and manipulation to establish dominance and superiority. It even deceives itself because of its extreme pride and arrogance. This further causes it to believe it is above the law.

When man exhibits hubris, it is regarded as a defining characteristic of the antichrist's rebellion against God.

Pride and arrogance are the fundamental weaknesses that will inevitably lead to man's demise. It blinds him to his own limitations. He will elevate himself above anything that is called God or worshiped. Thessalonians 2:4, for instance, says, "He will oppose and will exalt himself over everything that is called God or is worshiped, so that he sets himself up in God's temple, proclaiming himself to be God." Without ethical considerations to guide him, he will overstep his moral boundaries.

In Daniel, Chapter 3 of the Holy Bible, King Nebuchadnezzar of Babylon created a golden image of himself. This image was meant to be worshipped by all. He summoned all of Babylon's officials, from princes to sheriffs, to the dedication of the idol he created of himself. When the moment came, everyone would bow down and worship the image. Failure to obey this order would result in death by burning in a furnace of fire.

Three of his officials, Shadrach, Meshach, and Abednego refused to prostrate before his golden image. They told him that they serve the true and living God. They informed him that they would not worship his Babylonian gods or worship the golden image that he created of himself. They informed him that the true and living God would deliver them from his fire. So King Nebuchadnezzar enraged and filled with the spirit of the antichrist, ordered that the furnace be heated seven times hotter than it was already. Then he commanded the mightiest men in his army to bind and toss them into the furnace. The fire was so intense that it killed the mighty men who hurled them into the furnace.

However, God is faithful, and he not only saved Shadrach, Meshach, and Abednego, but he also went into the fire with them. How good is our Lord and Savior Jesus Christ, who will go into the fire with us when we are faithful to him! King Nebuchadnezzar was shocked at what he saw and asked "Didn't we throw three into the fire? Lo, I see four men loose, walking in the midst of the fire, and they have no hurt; and the fourth is like the Son of God." After the king called them out of the fire, they didn't even smell like smoke! See, King Nebuchadnezzar could have used this opportunity to ask them more about their God who gave them so much courage and boldness.

However, he was too caught up in himself and desired to be worshipped instead. Ultimately, God would bring King Nebuchadnezzar to recognize him as the true and living God. King Nebuchadnezzar would eventually lose his authority and sanity. Only after repenting with a sincere heart would God restore King Nebuchadnezzar's mind and position.

Antichrists position themselves to be as God. He will speak of himself as the sole person to solve the world's problems when only Christ can resolve the world's issues. An antichrist will typically find a scapegoat or enemy to direct the people's focus. Usually, it's the less fortunate, a minority, or a group with little power or influence. Once the poison of the hatred has been stirred up, the followers will do anything to appease the one instigating it.

This is a trick of the antichrist spirit and it causes "man" to stumble by being misled by lying, greedy, weak, self-serving, incapable, misguided narcissistic sociopaths, who are not for "We the People" but for me, myself, and I. Of which, God tells us to be wary. HE says,

"Beloved, believe not every spirit, but try the spirits whether they are of God: because many false prophets are gone out into the world. Hereby know ye the Spirit of God: Every spirit that confesses that Jesus Christ is come in the flesh is of God. And every spirit that confesses not that Jesus Christ has come in the flesh is not of God: and this is the spirit of antichrist, whereof ye have heard that it should come; and even now already is it in the world"

- 1 JOHN 4:1-3

The Lord Jesus Christ's Spirit gives assurance. In fact, the fruit of the Spirit is "love, joy, peace, patience, kindness, goodness, faithfulness, gentleness, and self-control." HIS Spirit doesn't mislead or lie. It doesn't deprive people of their most basic human rights or incite violence because of the result of a political party's failed election. God's Spirit doesn't point fingers when con-

fronted by the consequences of illegal actions. God's Spirit doesn't lie or manipulate.
God doesn't disregard others or try to erase
history. HE doesn't rip the fabric of society
to pieces by trying to manipulate economic
control, by ruling against the church, or by
destroying everything that is good, like dis-
solving the board of education, destroying
prolific literature, and history books, or even
dividing the country.

God does not step on our constitution or
bill of rights. He doesn't try to erode our civil
liberties, or free thought, or cause disparities
in wealth by an imbalance of resources set
upon a throne for only the wealthy and privi-
leged. The Holy Spirit's characteristics are
representative of Jesus Christ Himself. God
will always show himself as the True and
Living God. Ultimately, all antichrists from
the first to the last will acknowledge Christ
as the one true and living God. This is evident in Philippians 2:10-11 (NIV), which
states,

"that at the name of Jesus, every knee should bow, of those in heaven, and of those on earth, and of those under the earth, and that every tongue should confess that Jesus Christ is Lord, to the glory of God the Father."

God is all-powerful (omnipotent), all-knowing (omniscience), everywhere at the same time (omnipresent), and infinite (eternality). HE will not be mocked. HE is to be reverenced and regarded. HE is what man will never be.

HE IS LORD AND SAVIOR!

www.ingramcontent.com/pod-product-compliance
Lightning Source LLC
Chambersburg PA
CBHW060929140726
47996CB00001B/436